JUMBLE® CORONATION

A Crowning Achievement of Puzzles!

Henri Arnold,
Bob Lee,
David L. Hoyt
and Jeff Knurek

TRIUMPH BOOKS

This book is available in quantity at special discounts
for your group or organization.

For further information, con tact:
Triumph Books LLC
814 North Franklin Street
Chicago, Illinois 60610
Phone: (312) 337-0747
www.triumphbooks.com

Printed in U.S.A.

ISBN: 978-1-62937-976-0

Design by Sue Knopf

Contents

Classic Puzzles
1–25...Page 1

Daily Puzzles
26–160...Page 27

Challenger Puzzles
161–180...Page 163

Answers
Page 184

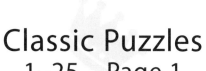

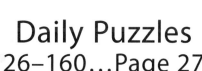

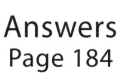

JUMBLE®
CORONATION

Classic Puzzles

PUZZLE

1

JUMBLE®

Unscramble these four Jumbles, one letter to each square, to form four ordinary words.

RYTUL

KADEB

SEJERY

PLINEP

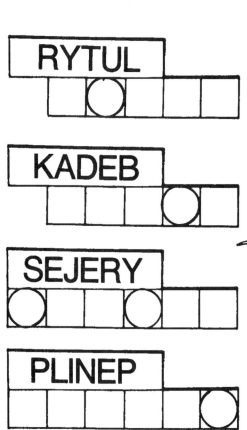

This'll wow 'em!
WHAT THE AUDIENCE GAVE HIM WHEN HE WAS EXPECTING CHEERS.

Now arrange the circled letters to form the surprise answer, as suggested by the above cartoon.

Print answer here

PUZZLE 2

JUMBLE®

Unscramble these four Jumbles, one letter to each square, to form four ordinary words.

VILEA

HUTOY

EWSUIN

DOMECY

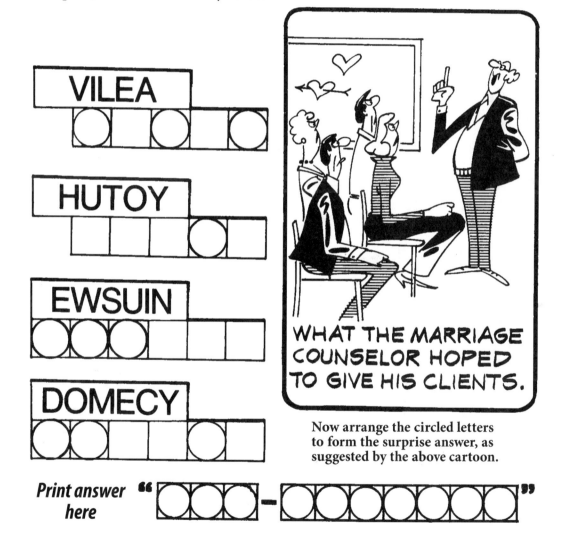

WHAT THE MARRIAGE COUNSELOR HOPED TO GIVE HIS CLIENTS.

Now arrange the circled letters to form the surprise answer, as suggested by the above cartoon.

Print answer here "○○○-○○○○○○○"

PUZZLE 3

JUMBLE®

Unscramble these four Jumbles, one letter to each square, to form four ordinary words.

KALCH

ZUFYZ

YAUBET

RICION

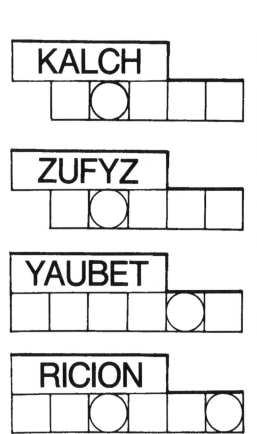

Hey, buddy...
WHAT A SUCCESSFUL BORROWER HAS TO HAVE A GOOD SENSE OF.

Now arrange the circled letters to form the surprise answer, as suggested by the above cartoon.

Print answer here " "

JUMBLE®

Unscramble these four Jumbles, one letter to each square, to form four ordinary words.

DYSAN

NUWDE

URREBB

STIJUR

WHAT A DUDE SOMETIMES BECOMES AFTER MARRIAGE.

Now arrange the circled letters to form the surprise answer, as suggested by the above cartoon.

Print answer here " ___ - ____ "

PUZZLE

5

JUMBLE®

Unscramble these four Jumbles, one letter to each square, to form four ordinary words.

ANCKK

BUICC

NYWIRT

SCAFIO

These will rest your eyes
But what will they do to my good looks?
WHAT CONCEIT MIGHT BE A FORM OF.

Now arrange the circled letters to form the surprise answer, as suggested by the above cartoon.

Print answer here " - "

PUZZLE

6

JUMBLE®

Unscramble these four Jumbles, one letter to each square, to form four ordinary words.

YARPH

NAPAG

JOOUSY

CATATH

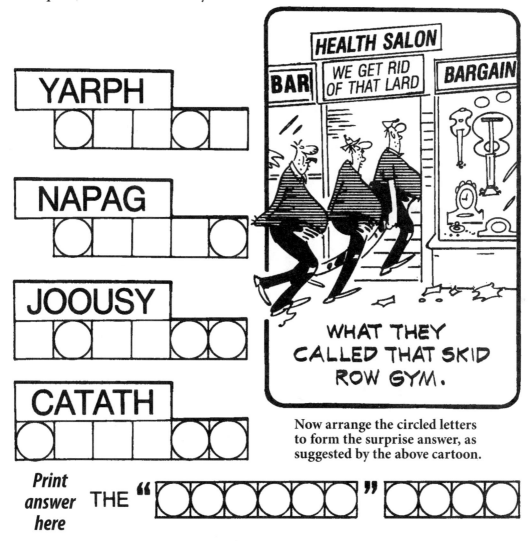

HEALTH SALON
BAR
WE GET RID OF THAT LARD
BARGAIN
WHAT THEY CALLED THAT SKID ROW GYM.

Now arrange the circled letters to form the surprise answer, as suggested by the above cartoon.

Print answer here THE " "

JUMBLE®

Unscramble these four Jumbles, one letter to each square, to form four ordinary words.

QASUW

HECEK

NAHDEL

ENBRAY

Now you're "in"
HOW A CONFORMIST USUALLY DOES THINGS.

Now arrange the circled letters to form the surprise answer, as suggested by the above cartoon.

Print answer here THE " ◯◯◯◯ " ◯◯◯

JUMBLE®

Unscramble these four Jumbles, one letter to each square, to form four ordinary words.

SABUQ

BOBAT

DRUENE

TRAULB

He'll never see that money again
You can say that again!
$

WHAT YOU MIGHT CALL A GUY WHO NEVER PAYS WHAT HE OWES.

Now arrange the circled letters to form the surprise answer, as suggested by the above cartoon.

Print answer here A "◯◯◯◯◯" ◯◯◯◯◯

PUZZLE

9

JUMBLE®

Unscramble these four Jumbles, one letter to each square, to form four ordinary words.

PIMSK

DEKEY

TIVNAY

SOLFIS

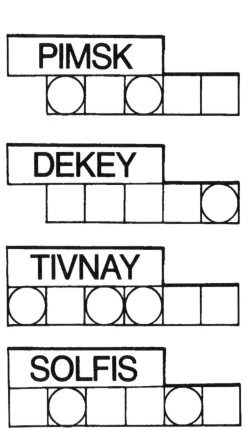

HOW SOME CREATURES "MULTIPLY."

Now arrange the circled letters to form the surprise answer, as suggested by the above cartoon.

Print answer here BY " "

PUZZLE

10

JUMBLE®

Unscramble these four Jumbles, one letter to each square, to form four ordinary words.

HECKT

NARFC

ZYNEEM

NAIFEL

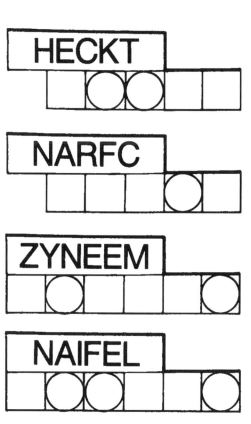

Go ahead, son, it's your duty—and privilege
VOTE HERE

WHAT IS A YOUNG MAN GOING TO BE AFTER HE REACHES EIGHTEEN?

Now arrange the circled letters to form the surprise answer, as suggested by the above cartoon.

Print answer here

JUMBLE®

Unscramble these four Jumbles, one letter to each square, to form four ordinary words.

HORTT

YERNT

AJURAG

KRUBEE

Sad news?
WHAT THAT STORY ABOUT THE ONION CROP WAS.

Now arrange the circled letters to form the surprise answer, as suggested by the above cartoon.

Print answer here A

JUMBLE®

Unscramble these four Jumbles, one letter to each square, to form four ordinary words.

LARNS

OFTUL

YEARTT

INBOAL

She didn't want to stay single
IT'S BETTER TO LOVE A SHORT GUY THAN THIS.

Now arrange the circled letters to form the surprise answer, as suggested by the above cartoon.

Print answer here

PUZZLE

13

JUMBLE®

Unscramble these four Jumbles, one letter to each square, to form four ordinary words.

ONSOW

SAYGS

AGNEET

FAINAR

THE MAIN COURSE AT THE COMEDIANS' ANNUAL BANQUET.

Now arrange the circled letters to form the surprise answer, as suggested by the above cartoon.

Print answer here THE " "

PUZZLE 14

JUMBLE®

Unscramble these four Jumbles, one letter to each square, to form four ordinary words.

ALLAM

GRUPE

MINKOO

FLAMEE

WHAT THE BASEBALL THAT HIT THE DENTIST'S OFFICE WAS.

Now arrange the circled letters to form the surprise answer, as suggested by the above cartoon.

Print answer here THE "◯◯◯◯" ◯◯◯◯◯◯

JUMBLE®

Unscramble these four Jumbles, one letter to each square, to form four ordinary words.

DEXUE

LUBLY

CISNEC

JORNAG

IT TAKES GOOD MANNERS TO PUT UP WITH THIS.

Now arrange the circled letters to form the surprise answer, as suggested by the above cartoon.

Print answer here

JUMBLE®

Unscramble these four Jumbles, one letter to each square, to form four ordinary words.

LAWRB

INHEW

MARROD

SYPEDE

FOR A CONSCIENTIOUS DIETER THIS SHOULD BE SUFFICIENT.

Now arrange the circled letters to form the surprise answer, as suggested by the above cartoon.

Print answer here A ◯◯◯◯ TO THE "◯◯◯◯◯◯"

PUZZLE 17

JUMBLE®

Unscramble these four Jumbles, one letter to each square, to form four ordinary words.

YOOST

NOARP

TELBOT

DEGELP

Great storyteller
BOOKS
$
$
WHAT THE SUCCESSFUL AUTHOR'S NOVEL HAD.

Now arrange the circled letters to form the surprise answer, as suggested by the above cartoon.

Print answer here A " " OF

PUZZLE

18

JUMBLE®

Unscramble these four Jumbles, one letter to each square, to form four ordinary words.

OONNI

SYNOW

VAUDLE

TENNIV

Disturbing the peace
WHEN THE VIOLA PLAYER DISTURBED HIS NEIGHBORS LATE AT NIGHT, HE WAS ARRESTED FOR THIS.

Now arrange the circled letters to form the surprise answer, as suggested by the above cartoon.

Print answer here A "OOOOOO-OOOOO"

PUZZLE

19

JUMBLE®

Unscramble these four Jumbles, one letter to each square, to form four ordinary words.

NIFYN

CAPNI

PELSOG

BANACA

They say he makes a good living off sponging
A PERSON WHO SELDOM PAYS FRE-QUENTLY FINDS THAT THIS IS WHAT HIS LIFE STYLE DOES.

Now arrange the circled letters to form the surprise answer, as suggested by the above cartoon.

Print answer here “ ”

PUZZLE

20

JUMBLE®

Unscramble these four Jumbles, one letter to each square, to form four ordinary words.

TOFLY

BAIDE

GANOLS

LESTUS

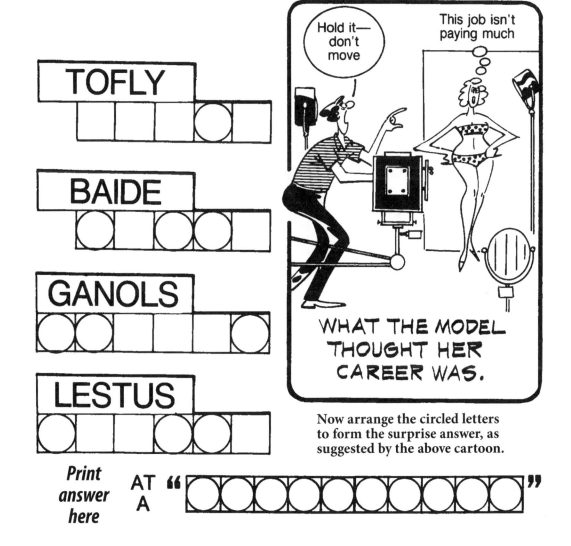

Hold it—don't move
This job isn't paying much
WHAT THE MODEL THOUGHT HER CAREER WAS.

Now arrange the circled letters to form the surprise answer, as suggested by the above cartoon.

Print answer here AT A “ ”

JUMBLE®

Unscramble these four Jumbles, one letter to each square, to form four ordinary words.

AMELY

TEPIN

COLUSH

MALORF

First, take my dog out
JUST MARRIED
WHAT HE GOT FROM REMARRIAGE.

Now arrange the circled letters to form the surprise answer, as suggested by the above cartoon.

Print answer here A NEW "" ON

PUZZLE

22

JUMBLE®

Unscramble these four Jumbles, one letter to each square, to form four ordinary words.

HEWIG

GLARN

DINTAB

LICKEF

WHETHER IT RAINED OR NOT THE WEATHER CASTER WAS THIS MOST OF THE TIME.

Now arrange the circled letters to form the surprise answer, as suggested by the above cartoon.

Print answer here

PUZZLE

23

JUMBLE®

Unscramble these four Jumbles, one letter to each square, to form four ordinary words.

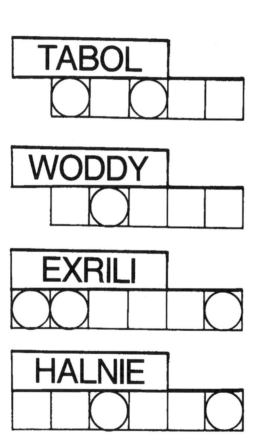

TABOL

WODDY

EXRILI

HALNIE

ANOTHER NAME FOR A YAWN.

Now arrange the circled letters to form the surprise answer, as suggested by the above cartoon.

Print answer here A ____ MADE BY A ____

JUMBLE®

Unscramble these four Jumbles, one letter to each square, to form four ordinary words.

SEHCS

CADYE

TIFLLE

NUMMIE

WHAT HE CALLED THOSE SONGS HE COMPOSED IN BED.

Now arrange the circled letters to form the surprise answer, as suggested by the above cartoon.

Print answer here

JUMBLE®

Unscramble these four Jumbles, one letter to each square, to form four ordinary words.

ALCAN

UNPER

NYGERT

GOIMES

But I do feel better
$ $ $
DOCTOR
IT TAKES MORE THAN THIS TO PAY AN ACUPUNCTURIST'S BILL.

Now arrange the circled letters to form the surprise answer, as suggested by the above cartoon.

Print answer here

JUMBLE®

CORONATION

Daily Puzzles

PUZZLE

26

JUMBLE®

Unscramble these four Jumbles, one letter to each square, to form four ordinary words.

DELOY

NAPOC

TOZALE

PREJUM

THAT RECKLESS CHAUFFEUR MUST HAVE HAD A LICENSE TO DRIVE —

Now arrange the circled letters to form the surprise answer, as suggested by the above cartoon.

Print answer here

PUZZLE 27

JUMBLE®

Unscramble these four Jumbles, one letter to each square, to form four ordinary words.

LUSKK

ROMAR

LANITE

DYLOOB

Can't understand a word he—or—they—
WHAT WOULD YOU EXPECT TO HEAR FROM A TWO-HEADED MONSTER?

Now arrange the circled letters to form the surprise answer, as suggested by the above cartoon.

Print answer here ______ - _____

JUMBLE®

Unscramble these four Jumbles, one letter to each square, to form four ordinary words.

URØCC

SCOUF

TUNBOY

CORNAY

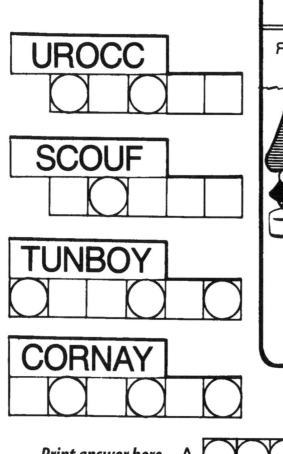

And one for my friend
BAR
WHAT HIS PAL THE SKELETON WAS.

Now arrange the circled letters to form the surprise answer, as suggested by the above cartoon.

Print answer here A

PUZZLE

29

JUMBLE®

Unscramble these four Jumbles, one letter to each square, to form four ordinary words.

WAKOE

LEROD

GITSAM

REFONZ

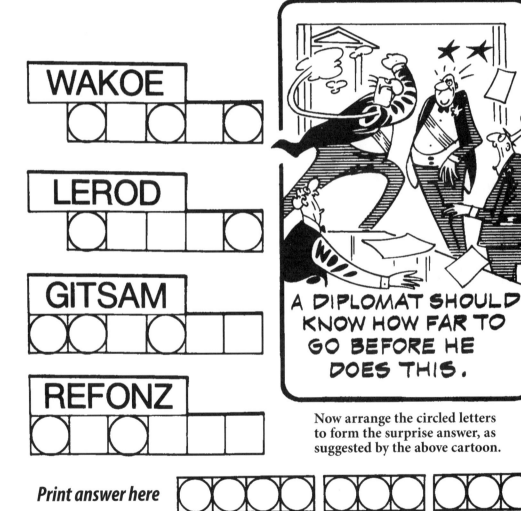

A DIPLOMAT SHOULD KNOW HOW FAR TO GO BEFORE HE DOES THIS.

Now arrange the circled letters to form the surprise answer, as suggested by the above cartoon.

Print answer here

JUMBLE®

Unscramble these four Jumbles, one letter to each square, to form four ordinary words.

POSOW

SELBS

TULFAY

RODINO

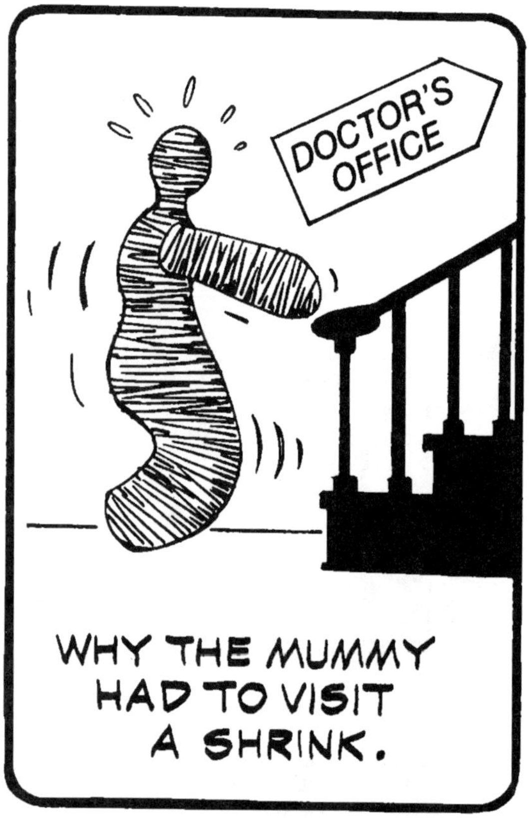
DOCTOR'S OFFICE
WHY THE MUMMY HAD TO VISIT A SHRINK.

Now arrange the circled letters to form the surprise answer, as suggested by the above cartoon.

Print answer here HE WAS ☐☐☐ ☐☐☐☐☐ UP

JUMBLE®

Unscramble these four Jumbles, one letter to each square, to form four ordinary words.

HOTOB

MAROA

RYSLIG

TROPSY

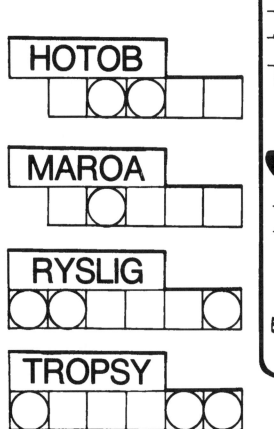

WHAT DRACULA'S BABY LIKED TO HEAR AT BEDTIME.

Now arrange the circled letters to form the surprise answer, as suggested by the above cartoon.

Print answer here A

PUZZLE 32

JUMBLE®

Unscramble these four Jumbles, one letter to each square, to form four ordinary words.

VALIA

WONIG

PAPNYS

GINPTY

WHAT WAS THE CONFIRMED BACHELOR'S SINGLE THOUGHT?

Now arrange the circled letters to form the surprise answer, as suggested by the above cartoon.

Print answer here ________ THAT ___

PUZZLE

33

JUMBLE®

Unscramble these four Jumbles, one letter to each square, to form four ordinary words.

INFEG

LABAN

ESSMYT

RELPHE

WHY THE MAGICIAN HIRED HER AS HIS ASSISTANT.

Now arrange the circled letters to form the surprise answer, as suggested by the above cartoon.

Print answer here

SHE WAS HIS ____-______

PUZZLE 34

JUMBLE®

Unscramble these four Jumbles, one letter to each square, to form four ordinary words.

HEWEL

TULSY

NEBATE

FIELDE

WHAT JUNIOR SAID ABOUT THE GAME, AFTER MOM MADE HIM A NEW BASE-BALL UNIFORM.

Now arrange the circled letters to form the surprise answer, as suggested by the above cartoon.

Print answer here IT'S "" UP

JUMBLE®

Unscramble these four Jumbles, one letter to each square, to form four ordinary words.

ENATE

DARRO

TENCED

SPICHY

P.D.
A DRIVER IS A GUY WHO FORGETS THAT HE USED TO BE THIS.

Now arrange the circled letters to form the surprise answer, as suggested by the above cartoon.

Print answer here A

JUMBLE®

Unscramble these four Jumbles, one letter to each square, to form four ordinary words.

SARBS

CREYM

STINCH

LUPHED

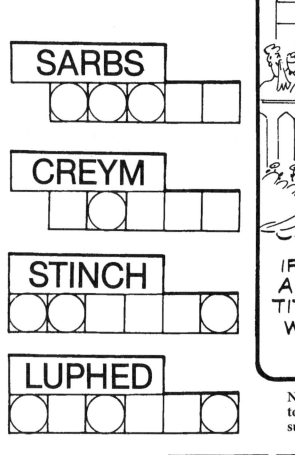

IF A MAN MARRIED A WOMAN WITH A TITLE OF NOBILITY, WHAT WOULD HE BE CALLED?

Now arrange the circled letters to form the surprise answer, as suggested by the above cartoon.

Print answer here

PUZZLE

37

JUMBLE®

Unscramble these four Jumbles, one letter to each square, to form four ordinary words.

TOHOB

GINOW

HOYNUL

FRIVED

Weren't you supposed to be out jogging today?
RACING
APPARENTLY THE EASIEST HABITS TO BREAK ARE THE ONES THAT ARE THIS.

Now arrange the circled letters to form the surprise answer, as suggested by the above cartoon.

Print answer here

PUZZLE 38

JUMBLE®

Unscramble these four Jumbles, one letter to each square, to form four ordinary words.

DYRYL

YUJIC

PUNCKA

ROBUGE

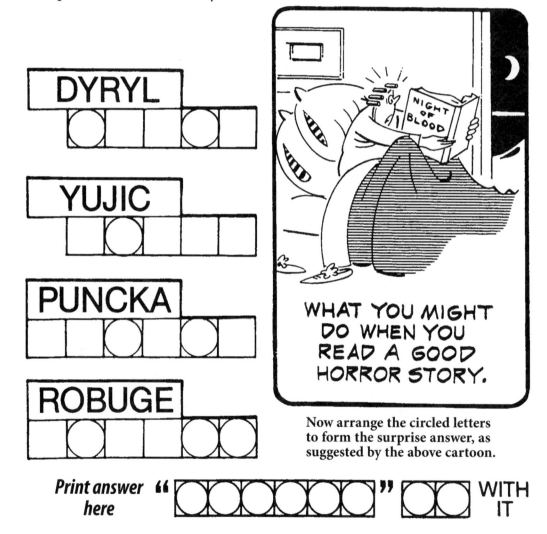

WHAT YOU MIGHT DO WHEN YOU READ A GOOD HORROR STORY.

Now arrange the circled letters to form the surprise answer, as suggested by the above cartoon.

Print answer here " " WITH IT

JUMBLE®

Unscramble these four Jumbles, one letter to each square, to form four ordinary words.

OGOIL

TOTID

DEKBEC

INJEYT

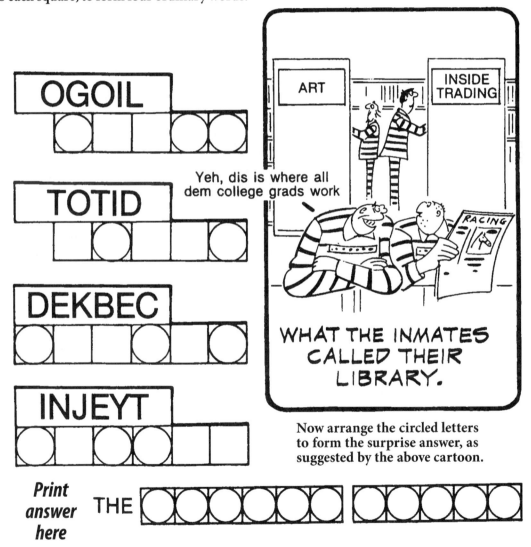

ART
INSIDE TRADING
Yeh, dis is where all dem college grads work
RACING

WHAT THE INMATES CALLED THEIR LIBRARY.

Now arrange the circled letters to form the surprise answer, as suggested by the above cartoon.

Print answer here THE

PUZZLE

40

JUMBLE®

Unscramble these four Jumbles, one letter to each square, to form four ordinary words.

BAXOR

FALEY

NEAFED

DOUSEX

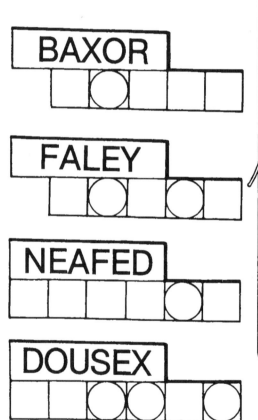

Remember your diet, dear

HE WAS TOLD TO EAT MORE SEAFOOD, SO NOW HE EATS EVERY TIME HE DOES THIS.

Now arrange the circled letters to form the surprise answer, as suggested by the above cartoon.

Print answer here

PUZZLE

41

JUMBLE®

Unscramble these four Jumbles, one letter to each square, to form four ordinary words.

JAROM

COVAL

IMSURT

PLATEA

It's now into the zillions!
THE SUM TOTAL OF OUR NATIONAL DEBT IS THIS.

Now arrange the circled letters to form the surprise answer, as suggested by the above cartoon.

Print answer here "☐☐☐☐ ☐☐☐☐☐!"

PUZZLE 42

JUMBLE®

Unscramble these four Jumbles, one letter to each square, to form four ordinary words.

TOLCH

USTEA

WENITH

OURSEA

THEY KEPT "MINUTES" AT THAT MEETING BUT MAN-AGED TO DO THIS.

Now arrange the circled letters to form the surprise answer, as suggested by the above cartoon.

Print answer here

PUZZLE

43

JUMBLE®

Unscramble these four Jumbles, one letter to each square, to form four ordinary words.

CANIP

DILEY

WHALLO

LAFTES

PET SHOP
IF YOU DON'T WANT YOUR DOG TO GET RUN OVER, BUY HIM THIS.

Now arrange the circled letters to form the surprise answer, as suggested by the above cartoon.

Print answer here A NEW "______" ON _____

PUZZLE

44

JUMBLE®

Unscramble these four Jumbles, one letter to each square, to form four ordinary words.

OVERP

BOTOR

YARQUR

RAMMOT

WHAT ALL THAT GOSSIP AT THE BOARDING HOUSE AMOUNTED TO.

Now arrange the circled letters to form the surprise answer, as suggested by the above cartoon.

Print answer here

PUZZLE

45

JUMBLE®

Unscramble these four Jumbles, one letter to each square, to form four ordinary words.

GAPAN

MEWNO

SPICET

GLANID

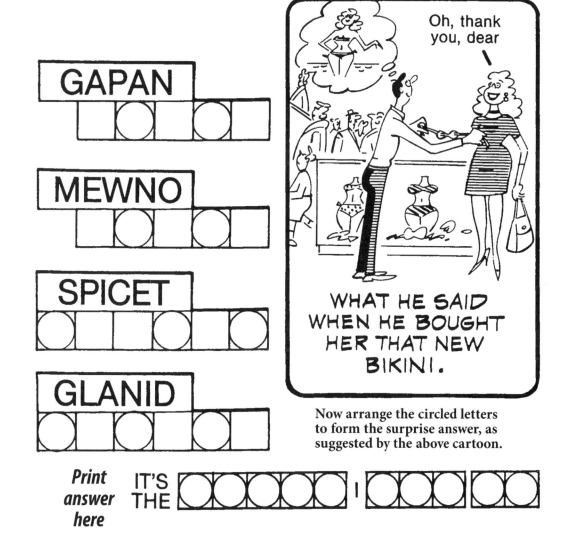

Oh, thank you, dear

WHAT HE SAID WHEN HE BOUGHT HER THAT NEW BIKINI.

Now arrange the circled letters to form the surprise answer, as suggested by the above cartoon.

Print answer here IT'S THE ______ ' ____ ___

PUZZLE

46

JUMBLE®

Unscramble these four Jumbles, one letter to each square, to form four ordinary words.

CAROK

RANEY

URQUOM

NOAWHY

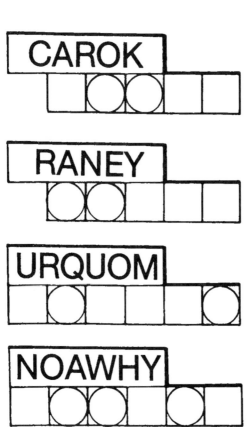

Please see my secretary on your way out
WHAT DO DOCTORS TAKE TO GET RID OF THE FLU?

Now arrange the circled letters to form the surprise answer, as suggested by the above cartoon.

Print answer here

JUMBLE®

Unscramble these four Jumbles, one letter to each square, to form four ordinary words.

DEPIT

MERFA

NIPICC

WHACES

And another thing...
SHE ROBBED HER HUSBAND OF HIS PEACE OF MIND BY CONSTANTLY GIVING HIM THIS.

Now arrange the circled letters to form the surprise answer, as suggested by the above cartoon.

Print answer here A ○○○○○ OF ○○○○

JUMBLE®

Unscramble these four Jumbles, one letter to each square, to form four ordinary words.

RUETT

FRAWE

SHUHRT

LEFZIZ

SALE
AT A BARGAIN COUNTER, THIS IS WHAT YOU GET.

Now arrange the circled letters to form the surprise answer, as suggested by the above cartoon.

Print answer here ◯◯◯◯ YOU "◯◯◯◯◯"

PUZZLE

49

JUMBLE®

Unscramble these four Jumbles, one letter to each square, to form four ordinary words.

GOLIC

NIRPT

COULIN

TISMEY

SOME POLITICIANS COULD HELP THEIR COUNTRY MORE BY GETTING THIS.

Now arrange the circled letters to form the surprise answer, as suggested by the above cartoon.

Print answer here ◯◯◯ OF ◯◯◯◯◯◯◯◯

PUZZLE

50

JUMBLE®

Unscramble these four Jumbles, one letter to each square, to form four ordinary words.

PEWID

SYBSA

DUNCEF

GAMIPE

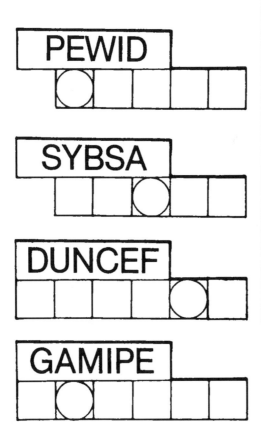

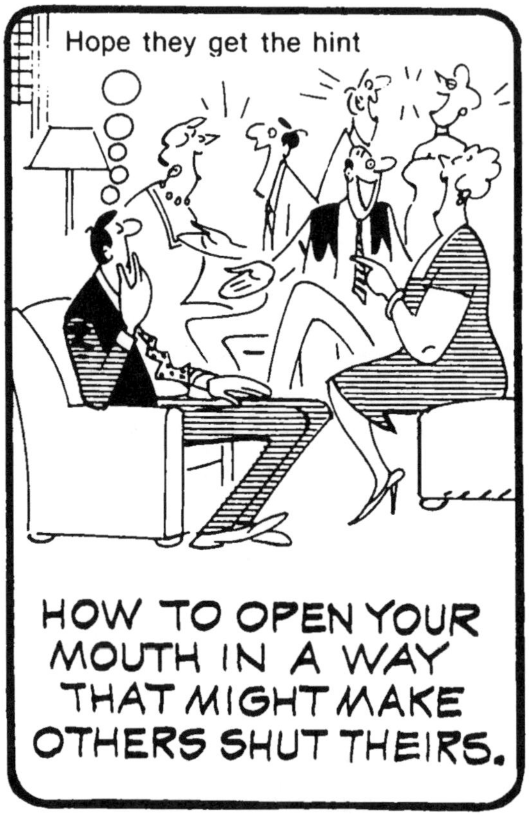

Hope they get the hint
HOW TO OPEN YOUR MOUTH IN A WAY THAT MIGHT MAKE OTHERS SHUT THEIRS.

Now arrange the circled letters to form the surprise answer, as suggested by the above cartoon.

Print answer here

PUZZLE

51

JUMBLE®

Unscramble these four Jumbles, one letter to each square, to form four ordinary words.

WEHIN

KNEAT

ANQUIT

SHRUPE

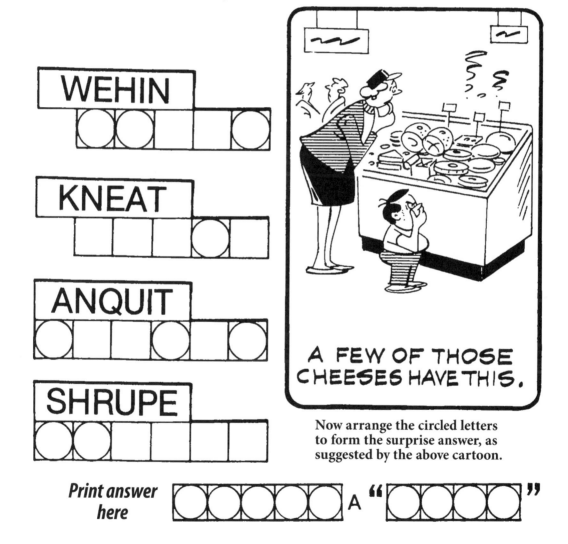

A FEW OF THOSE CHEESES HAVE THIS.

Now arrange the circled letters to form the surprise answer, as suggested by the above cartoon.

Print answer here A “ ”

PUZZLE

52

JUMBLE®

Unscramble these four Jumbles, one letter to each square, to form four ordinary words.

GERAW

HECKO

FALLOR

TYDWAR

WHAT A BIRD DOG MIGHT BE TRAINED FOR HUNTING IN.

Now arrange the circled letters to form the surprise answer, as suggested by the above cartoon.

Print answer here “ ”

PUZZLE

53

JUMBLE®

Unscramble these four Jumbles, one letter to each square, to form four ordinary words.

TOODU

SELIA

NOOBBA

PITTEO

Are you nuts? You'll never see that dough again
NEVER LEND MONEY TO THIS GUY!

Now arrange the circled letters to form the surprise answer, as suggested by the above cartoon.

Print answer here " "

JUMBLE®

Unscramble these four Jumbles, one letter to each square, to form four ordinary words.

TACCH

INGGO

LEVVET

BALIEW

Sorry, Rodney
A DATE IS SOMETHING YOU MUST BREAK WHEN YOU THIS.

Now arrange the circled letters to form the surprise answer, as suggested by the above cartoon.

Print answer here

JUMBLE®

Unscramble these four Jumbles, one letter to each square, to form four ordinary words.

BATHI

PERAP

LARCIA

GURDIT

A YOUNG PERSON MIGHT IMPROVE HIS EYESIGHT WHEN HE GETS THIS.

Now arrange the circled letters to form the surprise answer, as suggested by the above cartoon.

Print answer here

JUMBLE®

Unscramble these four Jumbles, one letter to each square, to form four ordinary words.

DATUL

SUGES

ORCEAN

SLUDON

Yes, dear you're right as usual
WHAT HE SAID HIS WIFE'S REASONING LARGELY WAS.

Now arrange the circled letters to form the surprise answer, as suggested by the above cartoon.

Print answer here " "

PUZZLE

57

JUMBLE®

Unscramble these four Jumbles, one letter to each square, to form four ordinary words.

SPEHE

VELGO

DYGOTS

GINDHI

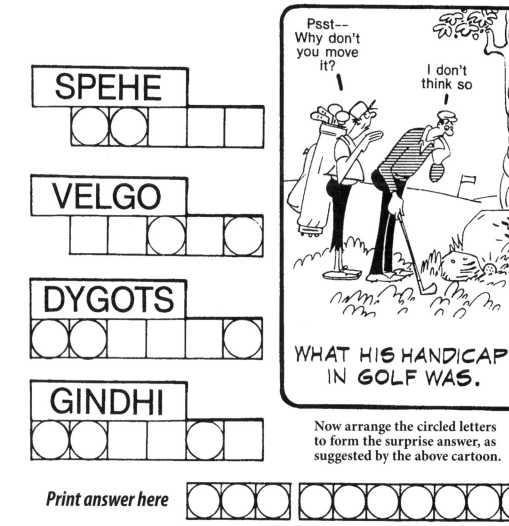

Psst-- Why don't you move it?
I don't think so
WHAT HIS HANDICAP IN GOLF WAS.

Now arrange the circled letters to form the surprise answer, as suggested by the above cartoon.

Print answer here

PUZZLE 58

JUMBLE®

Unscramble these four Jumbles, one letter to each square, to form four ordinary words.

ELTAM

RACCK

ARIVED

TEKLET

THERE WAS A LOT OF THIS IN THE WAITING ROOM OF THE EMPLOYMENT AGENCY.

Now arrange the circled letters to form the surprise answer, as suggested by the above cartoon.

Print answer here " "

PUZZLE 59

JUMBLE®

Unscramble these four Jumbles, one letter to each square, to form four ordinary words.

TAMID

CANYF

SLIMAD

GURTED

Welcome to our new lifetime member
WHAT THE LAWYER WHO JOINED THE NUDIST COLONY NEVER HAD.

Now arrange the circled letters to form the surprise answer, as suggested by the above cartoon.

Print answer here A "◯◯◯◯" ◯◯◯◯◯

PUZZLE

60

JUMBLE®

Unscramble these four Jumbles, one letter to each square, to form four ordinary words.

GALEL

JEECT

TENJUK

MINGOH

HE WHO LAUGHS LAST PROBABLY DOESN'T THIS.

Now arrange the circled letters to form the surprise answer, as suggested by the above cartoon.

Print answer here

JUMBLE®

Unscramble these four Jumbles, one letter to each square, to form four ordinary words.

YOVEC

NAGEM

PINDAK

RUTIVE

HE MARRIED HER
FOR HER LOOKS,
BUT NOT THIS.

Now arrange the circled letters to form the surprise answer, as suggested by the above cartoon.

Print answer here THE ☐☐☐☐ SHE OFTEN ☐☐☐☐☐ HIM

PUZZLE

62

JUMBLE®

Unscramble these four Jumbles, one letter to each square, to form four ordinary words.

NALBA

GUVEA

CAFUTE

HANKES

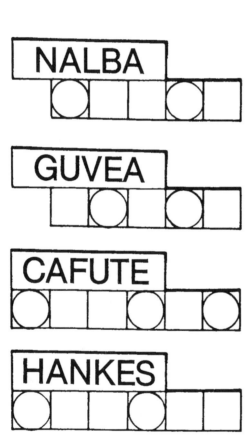

WHAT YOU CAN'T MAKE ON A SLOW HORSE.

Now arrange the circled letters to form the surprise answer, as suggested by the above cartoon.

Print answer here

JUMBLE®

Unscramble these four Jumbles, one letter to each square, to form four ordinary words.

HOPUC

TRYAR

SNODEC

CUPHIC

ANOTHER NAME FOR THAT REDUCING SALON.

Now arrange the circled letters to form the surprise answer, as suggested by the above cartoon.

Print answer here THE " "

PUZZLE

64

JUMBLE®

Unscramble these four Jumbles, one letter to each square, to form four ordinary words.

KNARC

HYNIS

YELMIT

SWEFET

OFTEN DROPPED BUT SELDOM PICKED UP.

Now arrange the circled letters to form the surprise answer, as suggested by the above cartoon.

Print answer here

JUMBLE®

Unscramble these four Jumbles, one letter to each square, to form four ordinary words.

FATOO

AXMMI

TANCAV

YAHNTS

WHAT THEY CALLED THAT WEALTHY PLAYBOY.

Now arrange the circled letters to form the surprise answer, as suggested by the above cartoon.

Print answer here “ - ”

PUZZLE

66

JUMBLE®

Unscramble these four Jumbles, one letter to each square, to form four ordinary words.

NYLOP

WETET

AHLEEX

SEDGIT

WHAT THE SENTRY AT THE ARMY KITCHEN KEPT.

Now arrange the circled letters to form the surprise answer, as suggested by the above cartoon.

Print answer here HIS “ ”

PUZZLE

67

JUMBLE®

Unscramble these four Jumbles, one letter to each square, to form four ordinary words.

MARAD

INSAB

GOOSTE

YASUNE

It's a long wait, but worth it
IS SHE A GOOD DRESSMAKER?

Now arrange the circled letters to form the surprise answer, as suggested by the above cartoon.

Print answer here

PUZZLE

68

JUMBLE®

Unscramble these four Jumbles, one letter to each square, to form four ordinary words.

DEYNE

CUNDE

LIFFUT

EMORCH

HE WAS A FRIEND OF THE OWNER WHICH IS WHY HE GOT EVERYTHING---

Now arrange the circled letters to form the surprise answer, as suggested by the above cartoon.

Print answer here " "

PUZZLE

69

JUMBLE®

Unscramble these four Jumbles, one letter to each square, to form four ordinary words.

CAMPH

TUILB

LIKLER

ERTOPY

WHAT THEY CALLED THOSE TWO PORCUPINES.

Now arrange the circled letters to form the surprise answer, as suggested by the above cartoon.

Print answer here A “ ”

PUZZLE

70

JUMBLE®

Unscramble these four Jumbles, one letter to each square, to form four ordinary words.

MENGO

JUTSO

KAUMPE

VEGASA

STICKS TO ONE THING AND HOPE-FULLY GETS THERE.

Now arrange the circled letters to form the surprise answer, as suggested by the above cartoon.

Print answer here

JUMBLE®

Unscramble these four Jumbles, one letter to each square, to form four ordinary words.

OUMID

NAJOB

CURSIC

PANPHE

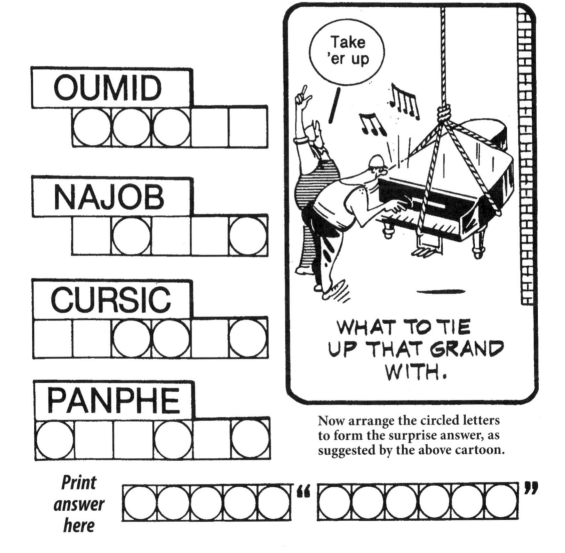

Take 'er up
WHAT TO TIE UP THAT GRAND WITH.

Now arrange the circled letters to form the surprise answer, as suggested by the above cartoon.

Print answer here "   "

PUZZLE 72

JUMBLE®

Unscramble these four Jumbles, one letter to each square, to form four ordinary words.

TREHB

ROLGY

VIEWLS

LOUHRY

WHAT THE RODEO PERFORMER DOES IN ORDER TO IMPRESS OTHERS.

Now arrange the circled letters to form the surprise answer, as suggested by the above cartoon.

Print answer here THE

PUZZLE

73

JUMBLE®

Unscramble these four Jumbles, one letter to each square, to form four ordinary words.

SEPOI

MIGRY

INCANE

DIRTOR

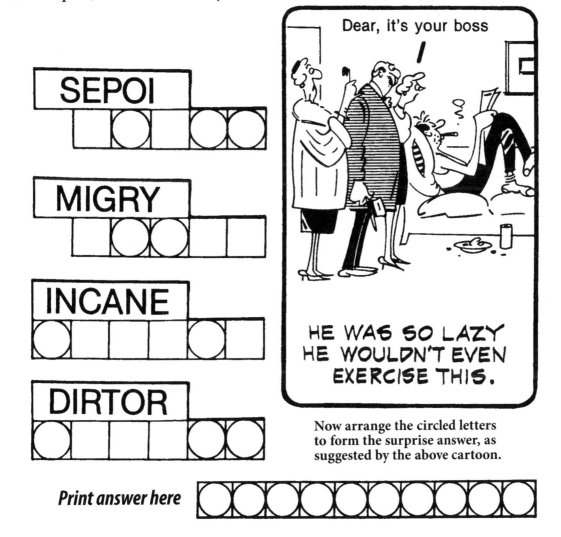

Dear, it's your boss

HE WAS SO LAZY HE WOULDN'T EVEN EXERCISE THIS.

Now arrange the circled letters to form the surprise answer, as suggested by the above cartoon.

Print answer here

PUZZLE 74

JUMBLE®

Unscramble these four Jumbles, one letter to each square, to form four ordinary words.

YARIN

PEBID

BOADUN

MARKEB

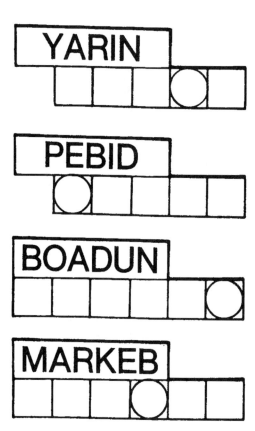

Can't stand those newfangled sounds
Should be agin the law
WHEN ROCK-'N'-ROLL WAS FIRST INTRODUCED, SOME OLD-TIMERS SAID IT SHOULD BE THIS.

Now arrange the circled letters to form the surprise answer, as suggested by the above cartoon.

Print answer here " "

JUMBLE®

Unscramble these four Jumbles, one letter to each square, to form four ordinary words.

BREEL

CONOR

DESEEC

UNTTAR

WHEN WILL THE MAIL ARRIVE?

Now arrange the circled letters to form the surprise answer, as suggested by the above cartoon.

Print answer here OR “ ”

PUZZLE

76

JUMBLE®

Unscramble these four Jumbles, one letter to each square, to form four ordinary words.

RICOU

BYNAD

CARPHE

MELFYS

WHAT DRY-AS-DUST PEOPLE NEVER SEEM TO DO.

Now arrange the circled letters to form the surprise answer, as suggested by the above cartoon.

Print answer here

JUMBLE®

Unscramble these four Jumbles, one letter to each square, to form four ordinary words.

ORPEN

NOVEY

RUSHOC

INDARC

WHAT KIDS GET
A BIG BANG
OUT OF.

Now arrange the circled letters to form the surprise answer, as suggested by the above cartoon.

Print answer here THE

PUZZLE

78

JUMBLE®

Unscramble these four Jumbles, one letter to each square, to form four ordinary words.

GINOR

◯◯□◯□

ENYAH

◯□□□◯

NITTEK

◯□◯◯□□

TORREC

□□◯□□◯

Maybe now they'll behave themselves

THEY'VE IMPROVED THE TRAINS TO WASHINGTON SO THAT THE POLITICIANS CAN NOW DO THIS.

Now arrange the circled letters to form the surprise answer, as suggested by the above cartoon.

Print answer here GET ON THE ◯◯◯◯◯ ◯◯◯◯◯

PUZZLE

79

JUMBLE®

Unscramble these four Jumbles, one letter to each square, to form four ordinary words.

TOBEG

UNSEE

BRAYNE

DIRAUM

SHE USED TO BE AFRAID OF MICE UNTIL SHE FINALLY DECIDED TO DO THIS.

Now arrange the circled letters to form the surprise answer, as suggested by the above cartoon.

Print answer here

PUZZLE

80

JUMBLE®

Unscramble these four Jumbles, one letter to each square, to form four ordinary words.

WILEH

TRAFE

BYSUIL

HUMBAS

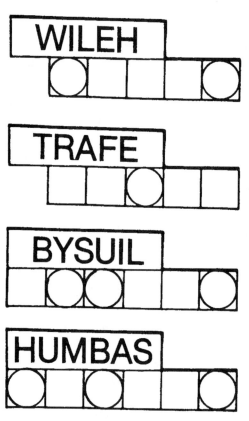

WHAT'S THAT UNDER-GROUND MOVEMENT THAT'S GOING ON IN MANY CITIES?

Now arrange the circled letters to form the surprise answer, as suggested by the above cartoon.

Print answer here

PUZZLE

81

JUMBLE®

Unscramble these four Jumbles, one letter to each square, to form four ordinary words.

TYKIT

BYGAG

NIPURT

AMRUTE

WALL ST.
ONE SURE WAY TO BEAT THE STOCK MARKET.

Now arrange the circled letters to form the surprise answer, as suggested by the above cartoon.

Print answer here JUST "_ _ _ _ _ _ _!"

PUZZLE

82

JUMBLE®

Unscramble these four Jumbles, one letter to each square, to form four ordinary words.

LAVEE

AUPSE

TERRFE

WARROH

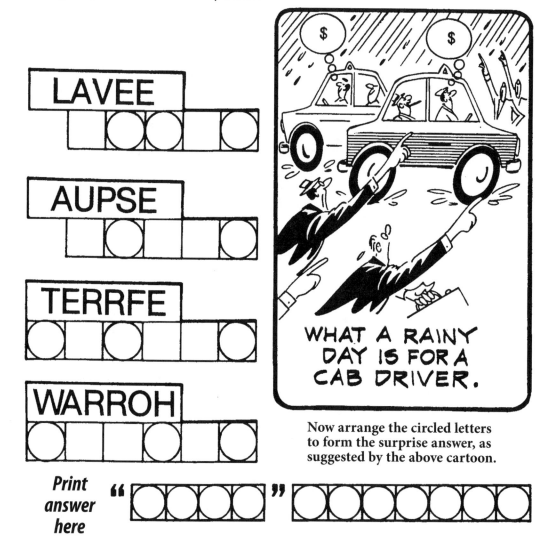

WHAT A RAINY DAY IS FOR A CAB DRIVER.

Now arrange the circled letters to form the surprise answer, as suggested by the above cartoon.

Print answer here “ ”

PUZZLE

83

JUMBLE®

Unscramble these four Jumbles, one letter to each square, to form four ordinary words.

ELVAT

RUHYR

PAWDUR

BISMUT

THE PESSIMIST WAS HANGING AROUND THE DELICATESSEN STORE BECAUSE HE WAS WAITING FOR THIS.

Now arrange the circled letters to form the surprise answer, as suggested by the above cartoon.

Print answer here “ ”

PUZZLE 84

JUMBLE®

Unscramble these four Jumbles, one letter to each square, to form four ordinary words.

FEBIT

UPYTT

VENAHE

LOWLAF

WHAT A GOOD POLICE DOG MIGHT PUT.

Now arrange the circled letters to form the surprise answer, as suggested by the above cartoon.

Print answer here INTO THE

PUZZLE

85

JUMBLE®

Unscramble these four Jumbles, one letter to each square, to form four ordinary words.

SUDOE

DOLOB

YALWEE

TRIAFY

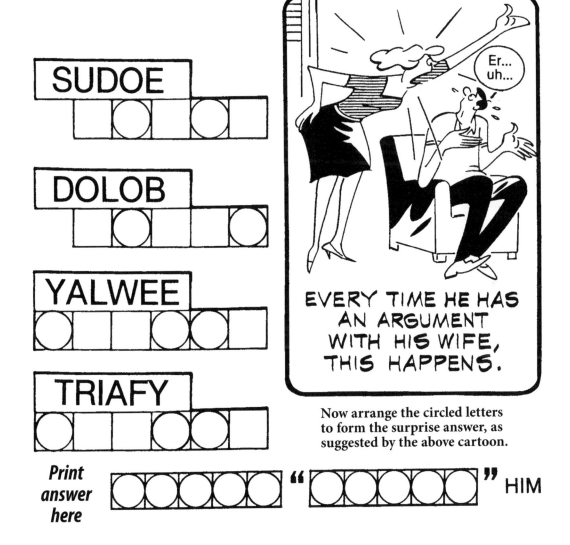

Er... uh...
EVERY TIME HE HAS AN ARGUMENT WITH HIS WIFE, THIS HAPPENS.

Now arrange the circled letters to form the surprise answer, as suggested by the above cartoon.

Print answer here “ ” HIM

PUZZLE

86

JUMBLE®

Unscramble these four Jumbles, one letter to each square, to form four ordinary words.

OSKET

ADDIE

NESSUC

CLOASE

WHAT THE SHIP'S DOCTORS GENERALLY DO.

Now arrange the circled letters to form the surprise answer, as suggested by the above cartoon.

Print answer here " "

PUZZLE

87

JUMBLE®

Unscramble these four Jumbles, one letter to each square, to form four ordinary words.

YOFAR

SHLYP

DULANO

NYLARX

IF YOU BECOME ADDICTED TO WRESTLING, IT MIGHT DO THIS.

Now arrange the circled letters to form the surprise answer, as suggested by the above cartoon.

Print answer here GET A ☐☐☐☐ ON ☐☐☐

PUZZLE

88

JUMBLE®

Unscramble these four Jumbles, one letter to each square, to form four ordinary words.

FIRGE

SUHOE

ORTETT

CUNNEA

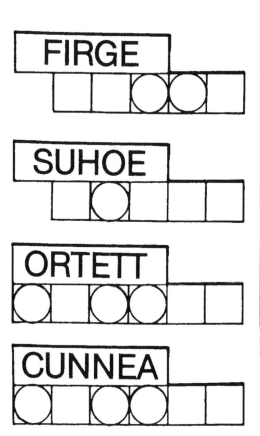

HE MARRIED A RICH WIFE, SO HE NEVER HAD TO PAY ANYTHING — EXCEPT THIS.

Now arrange the circled letters to form the surprise answer, as suggested by the above cartoon.

Print answer here

PUZZLE

89

JUMBLE®

Unscramble these four Jumbles, one letter to each square, to form four ordinary words.

VARGE

DOPKE

RUBETT

CLAISO

WHAT THE CANINE MEMBER OF THE BOY SCOUTS WAS CALLED.

Now arrange the circled letters to form the surprise answer, as suggested by the above cartoon.

Print answer here A " "

PUZZLE

90

JUMBLE®

Unscramble these four Jumbles, one letter to each square, to form four ordinary words.

THYIC

CEHKT

GUIFER

KLEACT

HE THOUGHT HE WAS A WIT, AND MOST OF THEM SAID HE WAS THIS.

Now arrange the circled letters to form the surprise answer, as suggested by the above cartoon.

Print answer here ◯◯◯◯ - ◯◯◯◯◯

PUZZLE

91

JUMBLE®

Unscramble these four Jumbles, one letter to each square, to form four ordinary words.

KLANB

TWAHR

YACENG

JOLTES

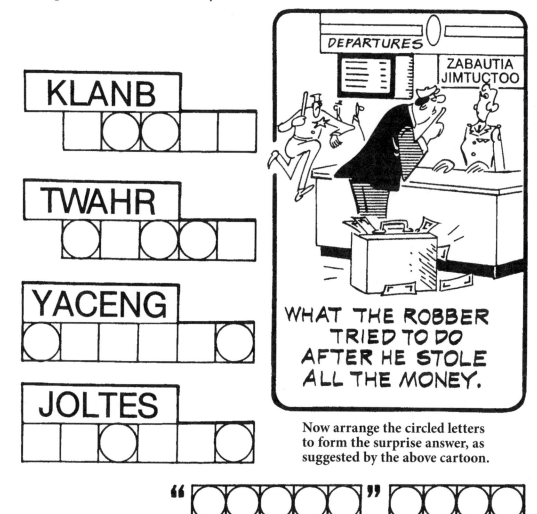

WHAT THE ROBBER TRIED TO DO AFTER HE STOLE ALL THE MONEY.

Now arrange the circled letters to form the surprise answer, as suggested by the above cartoon.

" ◯◯◯◯◯ " ◯◯◯◯

JUMBLE®

Unscramble these four Jumbles, one letter to each square, to form four ordinary words.

KNITH

PEROW

SURJIT

VURSCY

Now arrange the circled letters to form the surprise answer, as suggested by the above cartoon.

Print answer here "◯◯◯◯ THE ◯◯◯◯◯◯◯"

JUMBLE®

Unscramble these four Jumbles, one letter to each square, to form four ordinary words.

VERIP

SOINY

NEPPIS

ENCHIL

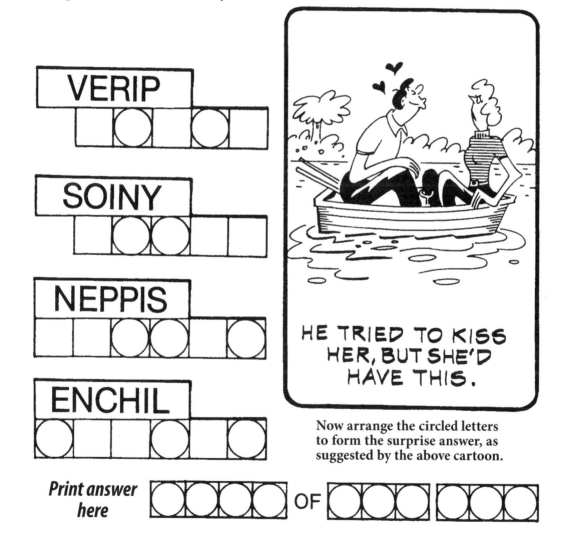

HE TRIED TO KISS HER, BUT SHE'D HAVE THIS.

Now arrange the circled letters to form the surprise answer, as suggested by the above cartoon.

Print answer here OF

PUZZLE

94

JUMBLE®

Unscramble these four Jumbles, one letter to each square, to form four ordinary words.

BISCA

TILUQ

DYOMLE

CAPTER

WHAT LACE
SHOULD NEVER BE.

Now arrange the circled letters to form the surprise answer, as suggested by the above cartoon.

Print answer here ☐☐☐ OF "☐-☐☐☐☐"

PUZZLE

95

JUMBLE®

Unscramble these four Jumbles, one letter to each square, to form four ordinary words.

GIRRO

WYSEN

SNUIGE

YIRRAT

BIGAMY IS
WHEN TWO---

Now arrange the circled letters to form the surprise answer, as suggested by the above cartoon.

Print answer here " _ _ _ _ _ " MAKE A _ _ _ _ _

JUMBLE®

Unscramble these four Jumbles, one letter to each square, to form four ordinary words.

AZERC

DEBIA

PITTSY

LOUBES

WHAT IGNORANCE AT THE BEACH IS.

Now arrange the circled letters to form the surprise answer, as suggested by the above cartoon.

Print answer here “ - ”

PUZZLE

97

JUMBLE®

Unscramble these four Jumbles, one letter to each square, to form four ordinary words.

DROAH

KRIPE

TEOGUN

HALINE

She has a good record

WHY THE BURLESQUE QUEEN DECIDED TO RUN FOR OFFICE.

Now arrange the circled letters to form the surprise answer, as suggested by the above cartoon.

Print answer here

SHE HAD ⃝⃝⃝⃝⃝⃝⃝ TO ⃝⃝⃝⃝

JUMBLE®

Unscramble these four Jumbles, one letter to each square, to form four ordinary words.

YOILD

ORRUJ

INVOIL

CHYSIP

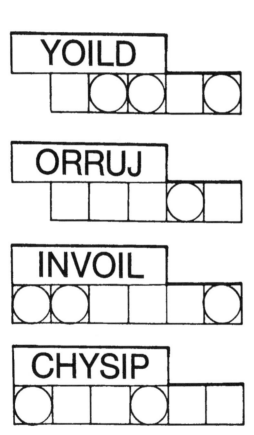

WHAT HAPPENS EVERY TIME HE TURNS OVER A NEW LEAF?

Now arrange the circled letters to form the surprise answer, as suggested by the above cartoon.

Print answer here IT'S

JUMBLE®

Unscramble these four Jumbles, one letter to each square, to form four ordinary words.

VERBA

NOOLC

EUGLED

DAGOIA

THIS MIGHT HELP A GAMBLER WIN A GOOD DEAL OF CHIPS.

Now arrange the circled letters to form the surprise answer, as suggested by the above cartoon.

Print answer here

JUMBLE®

Unscramble these four Jumbles, one letter to each square, to form four ordinary words.

VENOL

SINUM

TOWPUN

GLUTLE

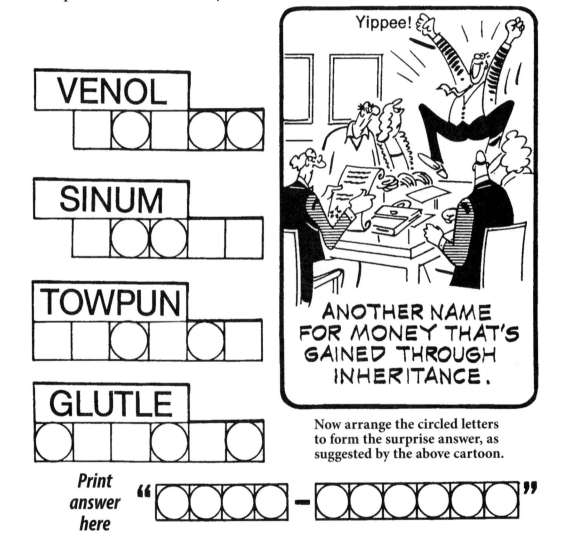

ANOTHER NAME FOR MONEY THAT'S GAINED THROUGH INHERITANCE.

Now arrange the circled letters to form the surprise answer, as suggested by the above cartoon.

Print answer here " - "

PUZZLE

101

JUMBLE®

Unscramble these four Jumbles, one letter to each square, to form four ordinary words.

OOCCA

NIORB

DORWYB

GLOANO

WHAT THE ACCORDIONIST'S CONCERT WAS.

Now arrange the circled letters to form the surprise answer, as suggested by the above cartoon.

Print answer here OUT

JUMBLE®

Unscramble these four Jumbles, one letter to each square, to form four ordinary words.

MONDE

YURST

SWERKE

FISHET

WHEN YOU TRY TO WASH A SMALL KID HE'S APT TO DO THIS.

Now arrange the circled letters to form the surprise answer, as suggested by the above cartoon.

Print answer here IT

PUZZLE 103

JUMBLE®

Unscramble these four Jumbles, one letter to each square, to form four ordinary words.

TUINY

ROUCS

KNABIG

PARMEC

SOME AGING THESPIANS MIGHT FIND IT DIFFICULT TO DO THIS.

Now arrange the circled letters to form the surprise answer, as suggested by the above cartoon.

Print answer here ◯◯◯ THEIR ◯◯◯

PUZZLE

104

JUMBLE®

Unscramble these four Jumbles, one letter to each square, to form four ordinary words.

PUTER

LOHLE

NUSIAD

LEYRAR

It took brains to get where he is
ONE WAY TO GET AHEAD AND STAY AHEAD IS TO DO THIS.

Now arrange the circled letters to form the surprise answer, as suggested by the above cartoon.

Print answer here

JUMBLE®

Unscramble these four Jumbles, one letter to each square, to form four ordinary words.

GUBOS

HASUQ

TESKUM

GLERCY

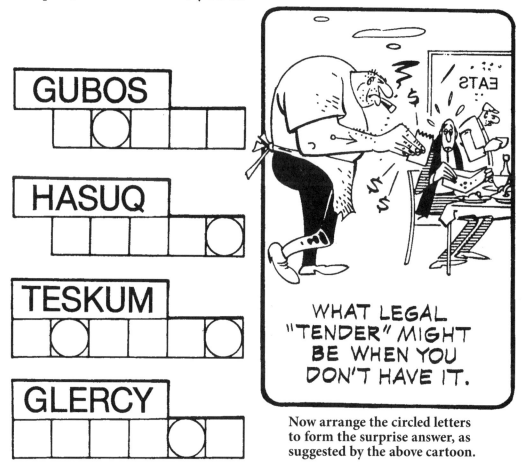

WHAT LEGAL "TENDER" MIGHT BE WHEN YOU DON'T HAVE IT.

Now arrange the circled letters to form the surprise answer, as suggested by the above cartoon.

Print answer here " "

PUZZLE

106

JUMBLE®

Unscramble these four Jumbles, one letter to each square, to form four ordinary words.

KUSHY

LAGIE

TAUBEY

BIMEBI

IN THOSE DAYS A WOMAN WOULD RAISE A HEM IN ORDER TO DO THIS.

Now arrange the circled letters to form the surprise answer, as suggested by the above cartoon.

Print answer here ___ ___ "___"

JUMBLE®

Unscramble these four Jumbles, one letter to each square, to form four ordinary words.

ARATO

GOARC

REDOWP

INROUJ

ANOTHER NAME FOR A CLOUDBURST.

Now arrange the circled letters to form the surprise answer, as suggested by the above cartoon.

Print answer here A " "

JUMBLE®

Unscramble these four Jumbles, one letter to each square, to form four ordinary words.

FELCT

ENAKO

INSHIF

SENFUI

IT WAS OFF-SEASON FOR FISHING, WHICH IS WHY THE SHERIFF MADE IT THIS.

Now arrange the circled letters to form the surprise answer, as suggested by the above cartoon.

Print answer here " - - "

PUZZLE

109

JUMBLE®

Unscramble these four Jumbles, one letter to each square, to form four ordinary words.

BEDRY

CLAWR

REBAVE

MANALY

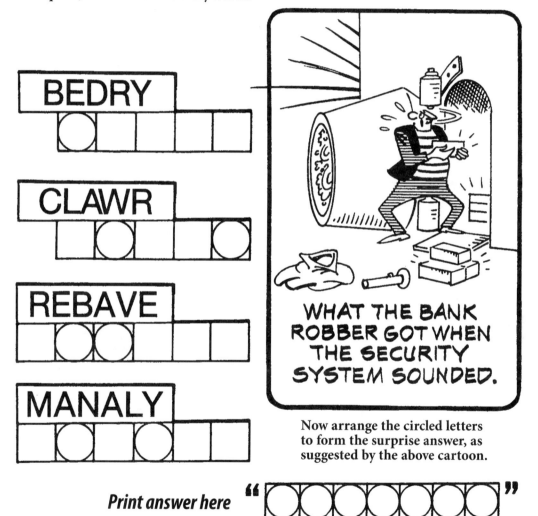

WHAT THE BANK ROBBER GOT WHEN THE SECURITY SYSTEM SOUNDED.

Now arrange the circled letters to form the surprise answer, as suggested by the above cartoon.

Print answer here “ ”

PUZZLE

110

JUMBLE®

Unscramble these four Jumbles, one letter to each square, to form four ordinary words.

LEAGE

YARIF

CLARNE

RALOPP

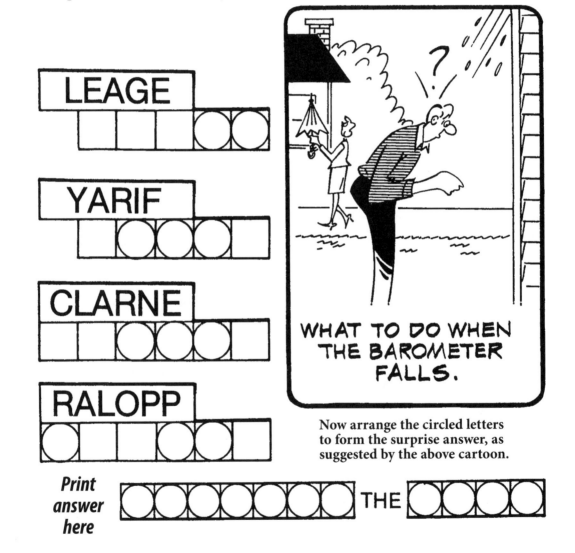

WHAT TO DO WHEN THE BAROMETER FALLS.

Now arrange the circled letters to form the surprise answer, as suggested by the above cartoon.

Print answer here THE

PUZZLE

111

JUMBLE®

Unscramble these four Jumbles, one letter to each square, to form four ordinary words.

VACHO

BBRUL

KENODY

LEAPAC

We're at a dead end. Now what?
Let's turn around and head to camp.
THE TRAIL THE TWINS WALKED ON HAD ENDED, SO THEY DECIDED TO ---

Now arrange the circled letters to form the surprise answer, as suggested by the above cartoon.

Print answer here

JUMBLE®

Unscramble these four Jumbles, one letter to each square, to form four ordinary words.

SMOTP

IRREV

UDONEF

PUNTEA

These give us so many wonderful things.
They are great.
WHEN THEY FIGURED OUT HOW TO GET SYRUP FROM MAPLES, IT WAS ---

Now arrange the circled letters to form the surprise answer, as suggested by the above cartoon.

Print answer here “ - ”

JUMBLE®

Unscramble these four Jumbles, one letter to each square, to form four ordinary words.

LIBUD

LATOG

CRUPES

SJYLUT

Most stars in our galaxy are red dwarfs. They can have habit-able planets.
Wow!
He makes it all so easy to understand.
WHEN NEIL DEGRASSE TYSON EXPLAINS STAR FORMATION, HE DOES A ---

Now arrange the circled letters to form the surprise answer, as suggested by the above cartoon.

Print answer here

PUZZLE

114

JUMBLE®

Unscramble these four Jumbles, one letter to each square, to form four ordinary words.

GHIMT

RTIDH

DEEDLP

FISHIN

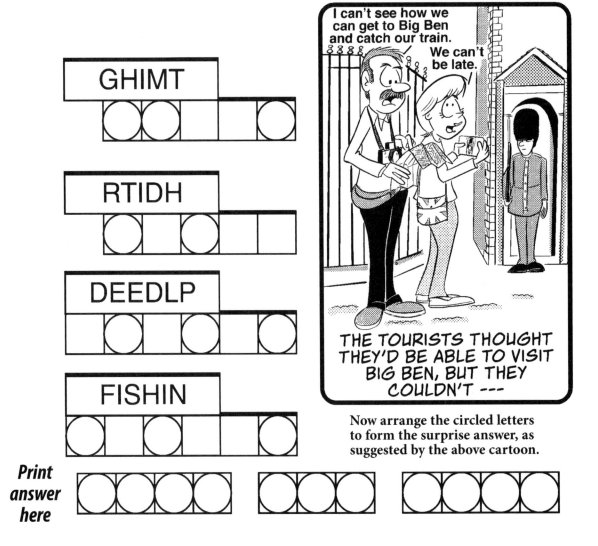

I can't see how we can get to Big Ben and catch our train.
We can't be late.
THE TOURISTS THOUGHT THEY'D BE ABLE TO VISIT BIG BEN, BUT THEY COULDN'T ---

Now arrange the circled letters to form the surprise answer, as suggested by the above cartoon.

Print answer here

PUZZLE

115

JUMBLE®

Unscramble these four Jumbles, one letter to each square, to form four ordinary words.

GACOR

FHERS

CAPTIN

MYIFAN

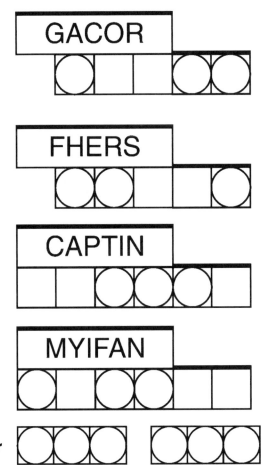

Ow! Are you sure these weren't made for Princess Elizabeth?
I am so sorry, Your Majesty.
GEORGE VI'S NEW SHOES WERE CAUSING HIM MUCH PAIN. THEY WERE ---

Now arrange the circled letters to form the surprise answer, as suggested by the above cartoon.

Print answer here

PUZZLE 116

JUMBLE®

Unscramble these four Jumbles, one letter to each square, to form four ordinary words.

SSYEA

NRUKT

KOIREO

KPACET

I'll take a six.
Draw me up a three, Mort.
I'll ink myself a three as well.
TO WRITE DOWN THEIR GOLF SCORES, THE CARTOONIST USED ---

Now arrange the circled letters to form the surprise answer, as suggested by the above cartoon.

Print answer here

PUZZLE 117

JUMBLE®

Unscramble these four Jumbles, one letter to each square, to form four ordinary words.

MUYTM

VAEWE

RONPEV

SIPRHM

Before we eat, let's have a moment of silence for our fellow soldiers who have made the ultimate sacrifice.
Happy Memo[...]ay
HE WAS A COOK IN THE MILITARY AND WAS PROUD TO ---

Now arrange the circled letters to form the surprise answer, as suggested by the above cartoon.

Print answer here

PUZZLE 118

JUMBLE®

Unscramble these four Jumbles, one letter to each square, to form four ordinary words.

OYNIS

CIGNI

RELHAB

TORETH

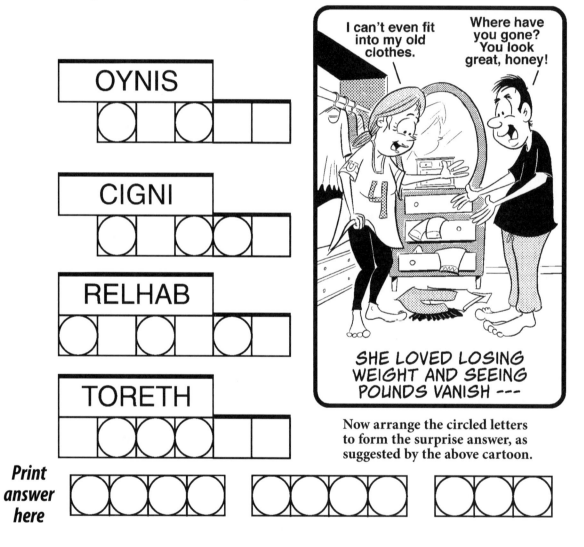

I can't even fit into my old clothes.
Where have you gone? You look great, honey!
SHE LOVED LOSING WEIGHT AND SEEING POUNDS VANISH ---

Now arrange the circled letters to form the surprise answer, as suggested by the above cartoon.

Print answer here

PUZZLE

119

JUMBLE®

Unscramble these four Jumbles, one letter to each square, to form four ordinary words.

LOYUS

AADNP

RZAHAD

NTENUL

Let's go! One more tug and we'll win!
Almost there!
His arms are strong.
SLEEPY HOLLOW'S INFAMOUS HORSEMAN WAS ABLE TO HELP HIS TUG-O-WAR TEAM ---

Now arrange the circled letters to form the surprise answer, as suggested by the above cartoon.

Print answer here

JUMBLE®

Unscramble these four Jumbles, one letter to each square, to form four ordinary words.

LAGCN

RYERB

FEYAST

SPIOME

Did you rip up the newspaper again?
Well, at least the Jumble didn't get ripped up.
QUESTIONING THE DOG ABOUT THE RIPPED-UP NEWSPAPER WAS ---

Now arrange the circled letters to form the surprise answer, as suggested by the above cartoon.

Print answer here "◯◯-◯◯◯◯-◯◯◯◯"

PUZZLE

121

JUMBLE®

Unscramble these four Jumbles, one letter to each square, to form four ordinary words.

THCCA

CIYTH

PRAROL

MREEEG

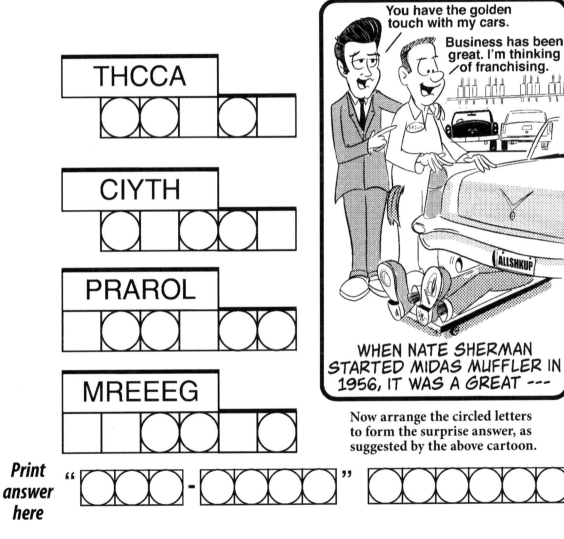

You have the golden touch with my cars.
Business has been great. I'm thinking of franchising.
ALLSHKUP
WHEN NATE SHERMAN STARTED MIDAS MUFFLER IN 1956, IT WAS A GREAT ---

Now arrange the circled letters to form the surprise answer, as suggested by the above cartoon.

Print answer here " ◯◯◯-◯◯◯◯ " ◯◯◯◯◯◯

PUZZLE

122

JUMBLE®

Unscramble these four Jumbles, one letter to each square, to form four ordinary words.

TOIPA

TOBDU

PRLIEP

WLEETV

Here's to us. We are our own bosses now.
We can go hiking to the summit, rock climbing, or just enjoy the view.

UPON RETIREMENT, THEY BUILT A MOUNTAINTOP DREAM HOME AND ---

Now arrange the circled letters to form the surprise answer, as suggested by the above cartoon.

Print answer here

PUZZLE

123

JUMBLE®

Unscramble these four Jumbles, one letter to each square, to form four ordinary words.

DWROL

SOBUG

RLIMYF

GUEHNO

Right here! Right now!
It's too crowded for this.
Let's go!
Not again.
HE CHALLENGED HIM TO ARM WRESTLE. NOW THEY JUST NEEDED SOME ---

Now arrange the circled letters to form the surprise answer, as suggested by the above cartoon.

Print answer here

JUMBLE®

Unscramble these four Jumbles, one letter to each square, to form four ordinary words.

GURHO

PINTE

TILNOO

DYIMAD

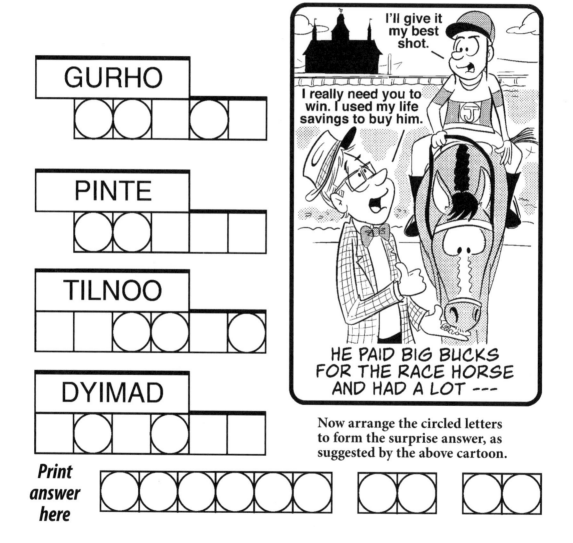

I'll give it my best shot.
I really need you to win. I used my life savings to buy him.
HE PAID BIG BUCKS FOR THE RACE HORSE AND HAD A LOT ---

Now arrange the circled letters to form the surprise answer, as suggested by the above cartoon.

Print answer here

PUZZLE

125

JUMBLE®

Unscramble these four Jumbles, one letter to each square, to form four ordinary words.

- TAWIA
- MHPTU
- VRSYUE
- THAYCC

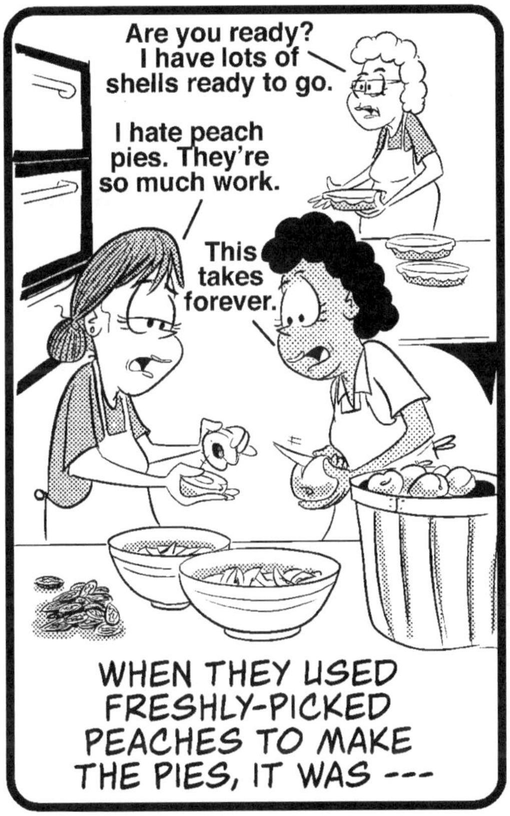

Are you ready? I have lots of shells ready to go.
I hate peach pies. They're so much work.
This takes forever.
WHEN THEY USED FRESHLY-PICKED PEACHES TO MAKE THE PIES, IT WAS ---

Now arrange the circled letters to form the surprise answer, as suggested by the above cartoon.

Print answer here

JUMBLE®

Unscramble these four Jumbles, one letter to each square, to form four ordinary words.

RIWTL

GEEWD

TOMHOS

VONGRE

How will we reach our rooms?
This is the end.
Let's go in the side entrance.
JIM MORRISON AND HIS BAND HAD SO MANY FANS, IT WAS DIFFICULT TO ---

Now arrange the circled letters to form the surprise answer, as suggested by the above cartoon.

Print answer here

PUZZLE

127

JUMBLE®

Unscramble these four Jumbles, one letter to each square, to form four ordinary words.

SYIRK

OSNOW

CAYNUL

NNIALD

Single file.
Watch your head.
TO ENTER THE CAVE WITH THE LOW ENTRANCE, THEY WOULD NEED ALL THEIR ---

Now arrange the circled letters to form the surprise answer, as suggested by the above cartoon.

Print answer here

PUZZLE

128

JUMBLE®

Unscramble these four Jumbles, one letter to each square, to form four ordinary words.

CUTHH

COFER

SASEWE

LEPTLE

I'm outta here!
Hey! That's my car!

WHEN THE CHICKEN CONVERTED THE OLD SPORTS CAR INTO A HELICOPTER, SHE ---

Now arrange the circled letters to form the surprise answer, as suggested by the above cartoon.

Print answer here

“ ”

PUZZLE

129

JUMBLE®

Unscramble these four Jumbles, one letter to each square, to form four ordinary words.

CUOST

LOEHL

TNYERD

RATMUI

What do you have there?
DEMETRIUS' DELI
It helps me keep track of how many lambs we've sold.

THE ANCIENT DELI USED THE ABACUS AT ITS ---

Now arrange the circled letters to form the surprise answer, as suggested by the above cartoon.

Print answer here

PUZZLE 130

JUMBLE®

Unscramble these four Jumbles, one letter to each square, to form four ordinary words.

GIRRO

UGGAE

LHEWAT

TAREHF

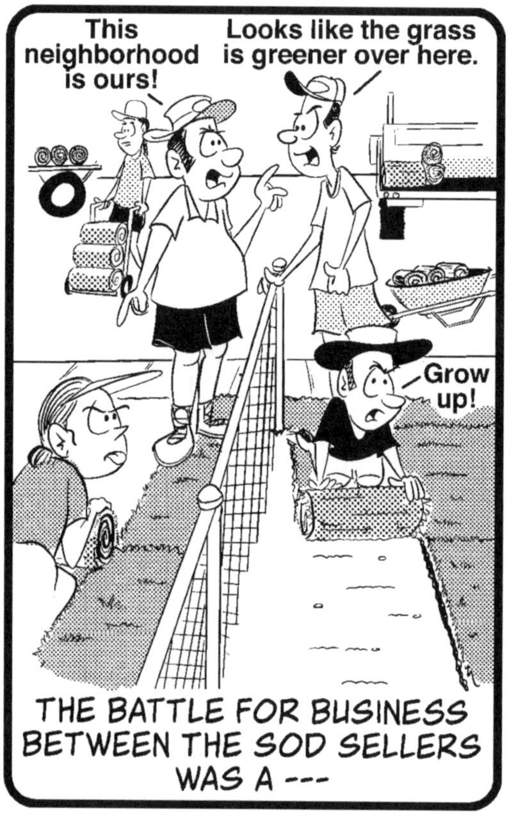

This neighborhood is ours!
Looks like the grass is greener over here.
Grow up!
THE BATTLE FOR BUSINESS BETWEEN THE SOD SELLERS WAS A ---

Now arrange the circled letters to form the surprise answer, as suggested by the above cartoon.

Print answer here

JUMBLE®

Unscramble these four Jumbles, one letter to each square, to form four ordinary words.

BIRON

SULYO

NETTAN

SARYAT

That's not something we're allowed to talk about.
How many guards are here on the island?
HOW MANY GUARDS PROTECT THE NEW YORK HARBOR STATUE? THEY'RE NOT ---

Now arrange the circled letters to form the surprise answer, as suggested by the above cartoon.

Print answer here

PUZZLE 132

JUMBLE®

Unscramble these four Jumbles, one letter to each square, to form four ordinary words.

CYDAE

LDANB

BONGOL

EYLLVA

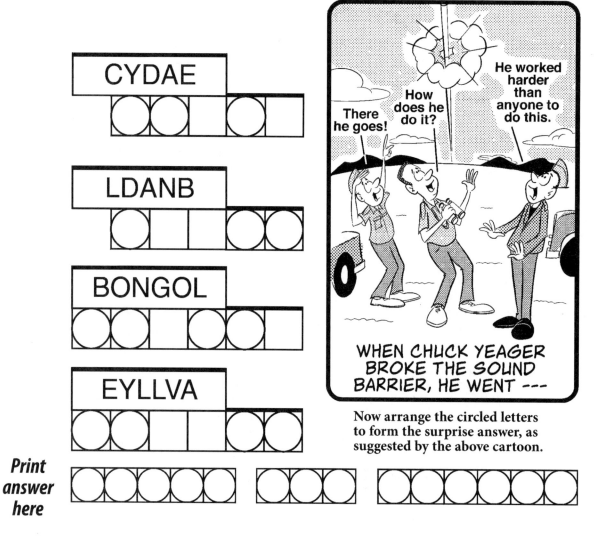

There he goes!
How does he do it?
He worked harder than anyone to do this.
WHEN CHUCK YEAGER BROKE THE SOUND BARRIER, HE WENT ---

Now arrange the circled letters to form the surprise answer, as suggested by the above cartoon.

Print answer here

PUZZLE

133

JUMBLE®

Unscramble these four Jumbles, one letter to each square, to form four ordinary words.

VAARL

WARND

TOPTEN

SYUBLI

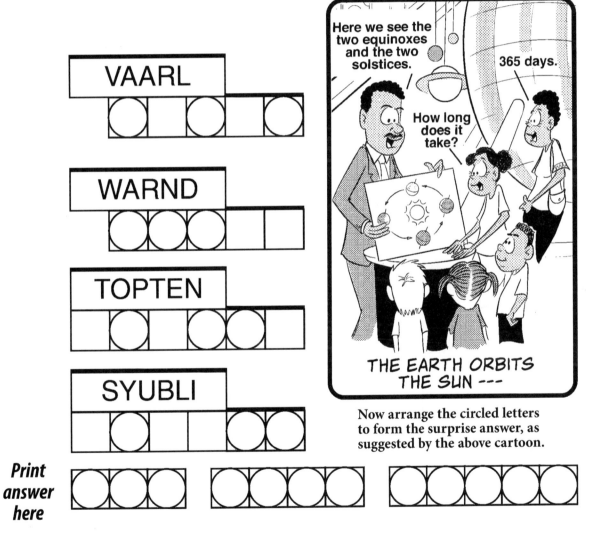

Here we see the two equinoxes and the two solstices.
How long does it take?
365 days.
THE EARTH ORBITS THE SUN ---

Now arrange the circled letters to form the surprise answer, as suggested by the above cartoon.

Print answer here

PUZZLE 134

JUMBLE®

Unscramble these four Jumbles, one letter to each square, to form four ordinary words.

PYMET

VTEEN

SARILP

CIPMAT

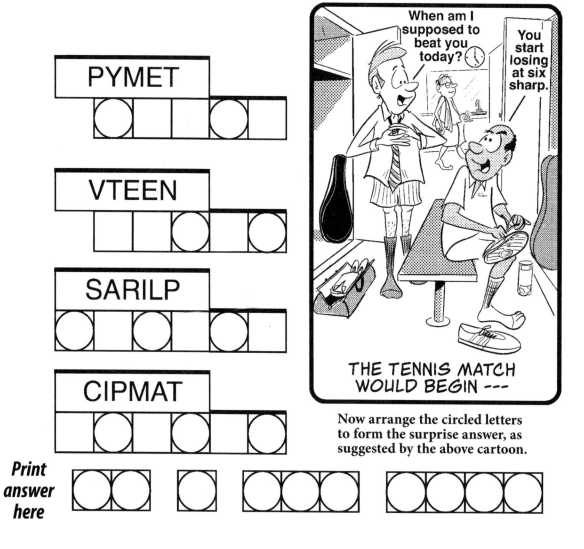

When am I supposed to beat you today?
You start losing at six sharp.
THE TENNIS MATCH WOULD BEGIN ---

Now arrange the circled letters to form the surprise answer, as suggested by the above cartoon.

Print answer here

PUZZLE 135

JUMBLE®

Unscramble these four Jumbles, one letter to each square, to form four ordinary words.

GITEN

SUNKK

PIATOU

ELMYIT

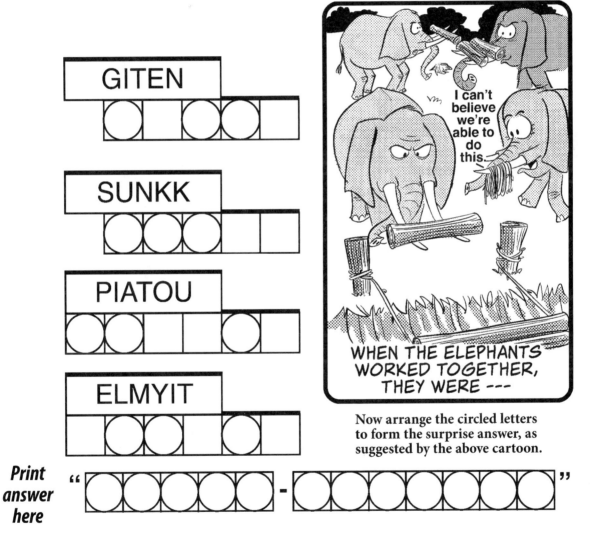

I can't believe we're able to do this.
WHEN THE ELEPHANTS WORKED TOGETHER, THEY WERE ---

Now arrange the circled letters to form the surprise answer, as suggested by the above cartoon.

Print answer here "   -   "

JUMBLE®

Unscramble these four Jumbles, one letter to each square, to form four ordinary words.

DORUG

LATFU

VISALH

NULBED

What do you say we head to the States for a tour?
Sure. Why not?
I'm in.
Maybe we can meet Elvis?
Yeah. Yeah. Yeah.
WHEN THE BEATLES WERE ASKED IF THEY WANTED TO TOUR AMERICA, THEY WERE ---

Now arrange the circled letters to form the surprise answer, as suggested by the above cartoon.

Print answer here

PUZZLE

137

JUMBLE®

Unscramble these four Jumbles, one letter to each square, to form four ordinary words.

POTZA

SUSGE

HGSITT

VOCNIE

This will deliver the medicine directly into your body. Are you ready?
You'll feel a slight pinch.
OK. Let's try this.
AFTER THE HYPODERMIC NEEDLE WAS PERFECTED, DOCTORS WERE READY TO ---

Now arrange the circled letters to form the surprise answer, as suggested by the above cartoon.

Print answer here

PUZZLE

138

JUMBLE®

Unscramble these four Jumbles, one letter to each square, to form four ordinary words.

LOPIS

NONOI

IRRRMO

GUTHAT

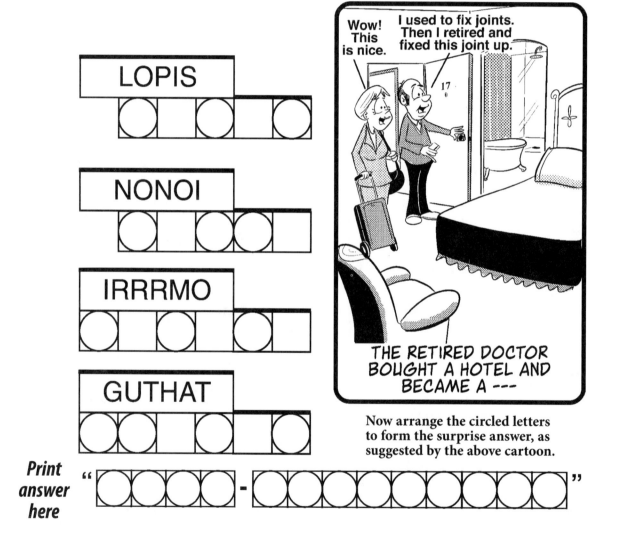

Wow! This is nice.
I used to fix joints. Then I retired and fixed this joint up.
17
THE RETIRED DOCTOR BOUGHT A HOTEL AND BECAME A ---

Now arrange the circled letters to form the surprise answer, as suggested by the above cartoon.

Print answer here "◯◯◯◯-◯◯◯◯◯◯◯◯◯"

PUZZLE

139

JUMBLE®

Unscramble these four Jumbles, one letter to each square, to form four ordinary words.

LIMEP

RGOOF

DSEDTO

CANENU

The voice makes vibrations onto the surface. Then the needle plays them back.
Your brain is solid! What amazing ideas you have.
Wow!
WHEN EDISON INVENTED THE PHONOGRAPH, THERE WAS NO DOUBT THAT HE WAS ---

Now arrange the circled letters to form the surprise answer, as suggested by the above cartoon.

Print answer here

JUMBLE®

Unscramble these four Jumbles, one letter to each square, to form four ordinary words.

GOLCI

NITEW

DEECRU

BRAJEB

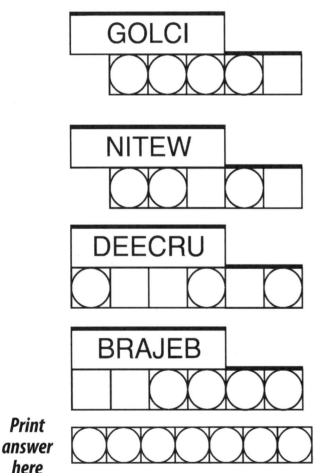

CAFFEINATION
We need to take him down!
I'm posting that his coffee is bitter.
Mr. Bean

WHEN ANOTHER COFFEE SHOP OPENED NEXT DOOR, THERE WAS ---

Now arrange the circled letters to form the surprise answer, as suggested by the above cartoon.

Print answer here

PUZZLE 141

JUMBLE®

Unscramble these four Jumbles, one letter to each square, to form four ordinary words.

CONTH

OFLCA

CETEND

CJLAAK

I'm thinking, why not score an opening and rivet on a ring to open it?
Wow! This certainly is patentable.
WHEN HE APPLIED FOR A PATENT ON HIS PULL-TAB INVENTION, THE PATENT OFFICE SAID ---

Now arrange the circled letters to form the surprise answer, as suggested by the above cartoon.

Print answer here

JUMBLE®

Unscramble these four Jumbles, one letter to each square, to form four ordinary words.

GHEED

OYRIN

GULOEN

GYEOAV

Grip it and rip it!
Whoa! You crushed it again!

NASCAR STAR KEVIN HARVICK LOVES GOLF AND PARTICULARLY ENJOYS A ---

Now arrange the circled letters to form the surprise answer, as suggested by the above cartoon.

Print answer here

PUZZLE

143

JUMBLE®

Unscramble these four Jumbles, one letter to each square, to form four ordinary words.

OZARR

UFDIL

GSUUFN

SREETJ

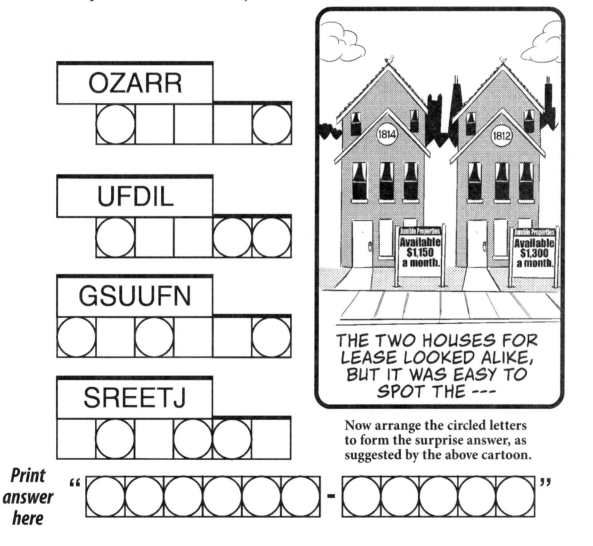

Now arrange the circled letters to form the surprise answer, as suggested by the above cartoon.

Print answer here " - "

PUZZLE

144

JUMBLE®

Unscramble these four Jumbles, one letter to each square, to form four ordinary words.

TTOEC

CIVEO

TYKONT

TFOHMA

It's so elegant here.
I love it, but I feel under-dressed.
THE NEW BISTRO WAS THE MOST ELEGANT IN TOWN, AND DINERS ---

Now arrange the circled letters to form the surprise answer, as suggested by the above cartoon.

Print answer here ____ A ______ __ __

JUMBLE®

Unscramble these four Jumbles, one letter to each square, to form four ordinary words.

IPNTU

YAMOF

WARELY

DEONLO

4:45! Right on schedule.
I love always being the first to see the sunrise.
West Quoddy Head
THE SUN HAS BEEN COMING UP IN THE EAST EVERY MORNING SINCE THE ---

Now arrange the circled letters to form the surprise answer, as suggested by the above cartoon.

Print answer here

PUZZLE

146

JUMBLE®

Unscramble these four Jumbles, one letter to each square, to form four ordinary words.

GEWIH

FNEOT

YUFTAL

BEEEFL

Nonsense! I made a fortune here and have lots in reserve.
Sorry we're shutting down, Boss.
DINOMNY
WITH THE OIL FIELD DEPLETED, THEY SHUT DOWN OPERATIONS. BUT THE OWNER WAS ---

Now arrange the circled letters to form the surprise answer, as suggested by the above cartoon.

Print answer here

PUZZLE 147

JUMBLE®

Unscramble these four Jumbles, one letter to each square, to form four ordinary words.

SUPEA

DUIMH

DLORCE

TEMMON

Why can't I open your door?
I can't get all my clothes in here.

WITH DIRTY CLOTHES EVERYWHERE, HER ATTEMPT TO CLEAN HER ROOM WAS BEING ---

Now arrange the circled letters to form the surprise answer, as suggested by the above cartoon.

Print answer here

PUZZLE

148

JUMBLE®

Unscramble these four Jumbles, one letter to each square, to form four ordinary words.

CATHW

RNIDG

MYITLE

TUONDL

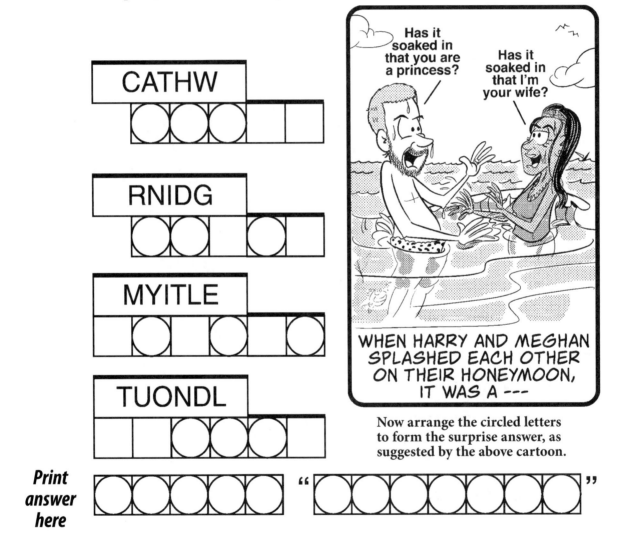

Has it soaked in that you are a princess?
Has it soaked in that I'm your wife?

WHEN HARRY AND MEGHAN SPLASHED EACH OTHER ON THEIR HONEYMOON, IT WAS A ---

Now arrange the circled letters to form the surprise answer, as suggested by the above cartoon.

Print answer here “ ”

PUZZLE

149

JUMBLE®

Unscramble these four Jumbles, one letter to each square, to form four ordinary words.

HACRI

ROBMO

GRAFLU

DEELTS

I've got drinks. Can you all bring some food?
No problem! I'll bring burgers.
I've got fireworks.
I'll bring salsa and chips.

WHEN ASKED TO HELP WITH HIS INDEPENDENCE DAY COOKOUT, HIS FRIENDS ---

Now arrange the circled letters to form the surprise answer, as suggested by the above cartoon.

Print answer here “ ”

PUZZLE

150

JUMBLE®

Unscramble these four Jumbles, one letter to each square, to form four ordinary words.

SSLAA

CNFEE

GNMINI

RIFDOB

Do you want to try my favorite hill?
I'll give it a shot.
RUNNING UP A HILLSIDE CAN BE GREAT EXERCISE IF YOU ARE ---

Now arrange the circled letters to form the surprise answer, as suggested by the above cartoon.

Print answer here

PUZZLE 151

JUMBLE®

Unscramble these four Jumbles, one letter to each square, to form four ordinary words.

PRAGH

RFAWH

PUYTED

BBOANO

Our tolls will generate enough money to pay back the bonds plus operational costs.
Toll Booths
Thank you for that explanation.

HER DETAILED EXPLANATION OF HOW THE TOLL MONEY WOULD BE USED WAS A ---

Now arrange the circled letters to form the surprise answer, as suggested by the above cartoon.

Print answer here "________-_____"

JUMBLE®

Unscramble these four Jumbles, one letter to each square, to form four ordinary words.

SLAOS

MIGER

LOWHOL

FRAISA

Land ho!
That's gotta make you happy, Captain.
Arrrr you kidding me?
Wait!
WHEN ASKED IF HE WAS HAPPY TO SPOT LAND, HE SAID ---

Now arrange the circled letters to form the surprise answer, as suggested by the above cartoon.

Print answer here ◯ "◯◯◯◯◯" ◯◯

JUMBLE®

Unscramble these four Jumbles, one letter to each square, to form four ordinary words.

MOUGB

AGGUE

BLDLAA

JADINO

He's so strong!
He put it up himself.
THE CARPENTER WAS VERY MUSCULAR, AND HIS ADMIRERS NOTICED HIS ---

Now arrange the circled letters to form the surprise answer, as suggested by the above cartoon.

Print answer here

PUZZLE

154

JUMBLE®

Unscramble these four Jumbles, one letter to each square, to form four ordinary words.

PUYSO

GORNP

ZAYNZS

TINKET

I didn't know I couldn't go around those cars.
They don't pay me enough!
Failed again?
LICENSE BU
NO PARKING
FAIL
WHEN HE FAILED THE DRIVING PORTION OF HIS DRIVER'S TEST, HE WAS IN A ---

Now arrange the circled letters to form the surprise answer, as suggested by the above cartoon.

Print answer here

JUMBLE®

Unscramble these four Jumbles, one letter to each square, to form four ordinary words.

YOFRE

RINLE

DALPED

GJWIAS

Wow! How did you think of this?
I figured, why not take a chair and put it on top of the horse?
I want one for my horse!

THE INVENTOR OF THE SADDLE HAD THE ---

Now arrange the circled letters to form the surprise answer, as suggested by the above cartoon.

Print answer here " ◯◯◯◯ " ◯◯◯◯

PUZZLE 156

JUMBLE®

Unscramble these four Jumbles, one letter to each square, to form four ordinary words.

CEEEM

KEIHR

SURBAD

SPUPHU

I've always wanted to be a bounty hunter. When I played hide-and-seek, I'd always find 'em.
You're hired. I'll train you.
WANTED
REWARD
WANTED
REWARD
REWARD
HE LONGED TO BE A BOUNTY HUNTER AND PLANNED TO ---

Now arrange the circled letters to form the surprise answer, as suggested by the above cartoon.

Print answer here

PUZZLE 157

JUMBLE®

Unscramble these four Jumbles, one letter to each square, to form four ordinary words.

TIDEY

TIGNL

SYLOGS

ANNETT

Was there any real justification for such a drastic price increase?
Yes. I needed a new yacht.
THE SHADY PHARMACEUTICAL EXECUTIVE'S PROFITS WERE---

Now arrange the circled letters to form the surprise answer, as suggested by the above cartoon.

Print answer here ___-______ _____

JUMBLE®

Unscramble these four Jumbles, one letter to each square, to form four ordinary words.

CCEHA

ZIMEA

HNETSC

TREESO

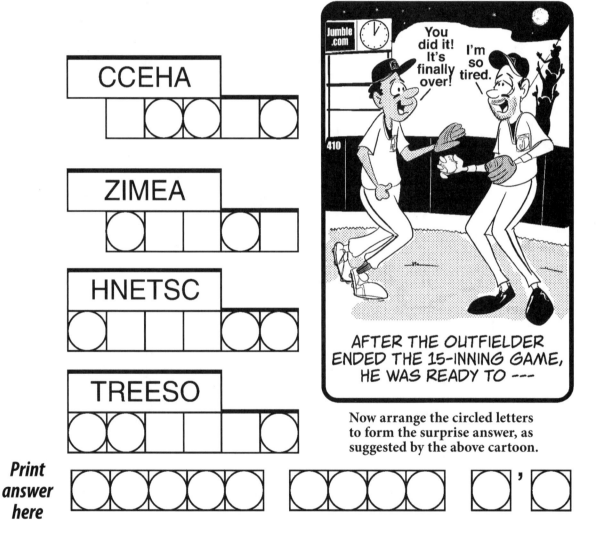

AFTER THE OUTFIELDER ENDED THE 15-INNING GAME, HE WAS READY TO ---

Now arrange the circled letters to form the surprise answer, as suggested by the above cartoon.

Print answer here

PUZZLE

159

JUMBLE®

Unscramble these four Jumbles, one letter to each square, to form four ordinary words.

STYXI

THEBR

NOBORC

GIJENL

Nine ball back into the corner, 13 ball in the side and then the eight ball in the corner for the win.
He's good!
He's the best.
VIP TABLE
WHEN IT CAME TO SHOWING OFF HIS ABILITY, THE POOL PLAYER WAS A ---

Now arrange the circled letters to form the surprise answer, as suggested by the above cartoon.

Print answer here

PUZZLE

160

JUMBLE®

Unscramble these four Jumbles, one letter to each square, to form four ordinary words.

NRTOF

SUDEO

SLEDOC

BLLOGA

It's traveled 3 billion miles in nine years and everything is working.
NASA
Is it true that it is going to leave our solar system?
WHEN THE SPACE PROBE APPROACHED PLUTO, MISSION CONTROL SAID ---

Now arrange the circled letters to form the surprise answer, as suggested by the above cartoon.

Print answer here

JUMBLE®
CORONATION

Challenger Puzzles

PUZZLE

161

JUMBLE®

Unscramble these six Jumbles, one letter to each square, to form six ordinary words.

HOCONH

PEOOSP

CDTTEE

CAMPIT

VALHIS

TROHET

Now arrange the circled letters to form the surprise answer, as suggested by the above cartoon.

Print answer here

ANSWER_START

ANSWER:

START

(removing scratch)

JUMBLE®

Unscramble these six Jumbles, one letter to each square, to form six ordinary words.

IRAWND

SISANG

NDUSED

HANELI

SITNLP

BOYEDM

You could retire if you let us buy your land.

No! I have to get back to work.

THE RECLUSE EXTRACTED GOLD WITHOUT ANY HELP AND LIKED TO ----

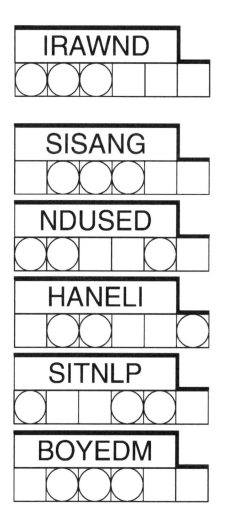

Now arrange the circled letters to form the surprise answer, as suggested by the above cartoon.

Print answer here

" ◯◯◯◯ " ◯◯◯ ◯◯◯ ◯◯◯◯◯◯◯

PUZZLE

163

JUMBLE®

Unscramble these six Jumbles, one letter to each square, to form six ordinary words.

MESSEA

VARSOY

MURMES

NUEVEA

VRRIED

MSSETY

Poetry Slam CHAMPIONSHIP
Here is our final matchup of the event.
You are no poet, and you know it.
You're going to frown when you go down.
THE POETRY COMPETITION FEATURED ---

Now arrange the circled letters to form the surprise answer, as suggested by the above cartoon.

Print answer here

PUZZLE

164

JUMBLE®

Unscramble these six Jumbles, one letter to each square, to form six ordinary words.

CORINI

MYGPUR

SIYFET

EFNODF

RUHOLY

GRIOIN

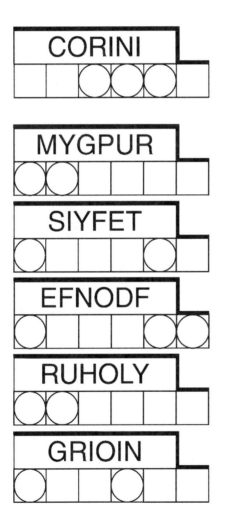

You can't count zero on your fingers.
Aa Bb Cc Dd Ee
=2
=1
=0
How many fingers is zero?
Use your thumb. It's not a finger.
A ZERO DOESN'T HAVE ANY VALUE BECAUSE IT'S ---

Now arrange the circled letters to form the surprise answer, as suggested by the above cartoon.

Print answer here

PUZZLE

165

JUMBLE®

Unscramble these six Jumbles, one letter to each square, to form six ordinary words.

GOONLB

CNACTE

ROMEAL

LEEUFY

WLIESV

TONKYT

That's right, Lukie! I'm your Da-Da!
Great! I'm the one feeding and changing him, and you get all the recognition.
Da-Da! Da-Da!
WHEN THE BABY'S FIRST WORDS WERE "DA-DA...DA-DA," THE FATHER EXCLAIMED ---

Now arrange the circled letters to form the surprise answer, as suggested by the above cartoon.

Print answer here

" ' '!

JUMBLE®

Unscramble these six Jumbles, one letter to each square, to form six ordinary words.

PEHHNY

FUTYFS

RMEEEG

RAYDLE

RNIHED

SLYOGS

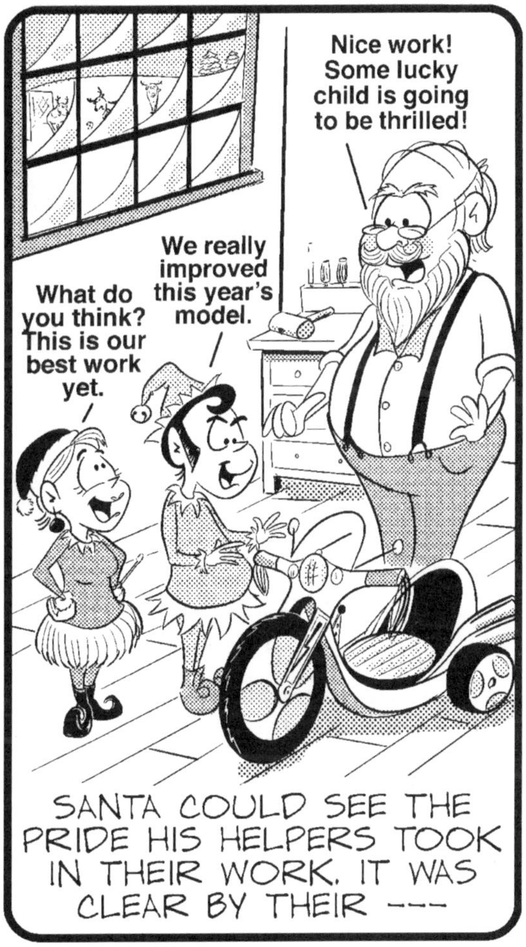
Nice work! Some lucky child is going to be thrilled!
We really improved this year's model.
What do you think? This is our best work yet.
SANTA COULD SEE THE PRIDE HIS HELPERS TOOK IN THEIR WORK. IT WAS CLEAR BY THEIR ---

Now arrange the circled letters to form the surprise answer, as suggested by the above cartoon.

Print answer here

◯◯◯◯ "◯◯◯" - ◯◯◯◯◯◯

JUMBLE®

Unscramble these six Jumbles, one letter to each square, to form six ordinary words.

MELTHE

FRAYDT

MMLEEB

BONDOY

RULPLA

TANDET

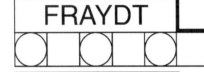

I've seen a lot of these lately. I'll give you two grand.
I've had three offers better than that.
JUMBLE

TO RAISE MONEY QUICKLY, THE ATHLETE SOLD HIS OLYMPIC GOLD BY PUTTING THE ---

Now arrange the circled letters to form the surprise answer, as suggested by the above cartoon.

Print answer here

" ○○○○○○ " ○○ ○○○ " ○○○○○ "

PUZZLE 168

JUMBLE®

Unscramble these six Jumbles, one letter to each square, to form six ordinary words.

DULHED

HERTTE

IDRAWN

NAYMIL

SAYILE

GAMEAD

WHEN ASKED WHEN SHE THOUGHT THE DRESS WOULD BE FINISHED, SHE ---

Now arrange the circled letters to form the surprise answer, as suggested by the above cartoon.

Print answer here

JUMBLE®

Unscramble these six Jumbles, one letter to each square, to form six ordinary words.

DAWORN

TNAMED

TXOPER

WHENPE

SORLIA

PCOYCU

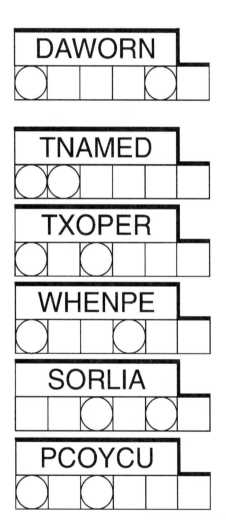

Could you jump in and help me in this neighborhood?
I'll take care of the cul-de-sacs.
FOR THE BUNNIES TO DELIVER THE EASTER EGGS TOGETHER, IT REQUIRED ---

Now arrange the circled letters to form the surprise answer, as suggested by the above cartoon.

Print answer here

" ◯◯ - ◯◯◯◯ - ◯◯◯◯◯◯◯◯◯ "

PUZZLE 170

JUMBLE®

Unscramble these six Jumbles, one letter to each square, to form six ordinary words.

NEGELT

WRECUF

SEDOXU

PYATNR

CCAIDI

GYILHH

Paula, will you be my first mate, for life?
I like the sound of that!

SHE LOVED THE WORDING OF HIS MARRIAGE PROPOSAL AND THOUGHT IT --

Now arrange the circled letters to form the surprise answer, as suggested by the above cartoon.

Print answer here

PUZZLE

171

JUMBLE®

Unscramble these six Jumbles, one letter to each square, to form six ordinary words.

ONNITO

ROLYHU

SEFTWE

MINTOO

MVOTIE

PETCID

You are so creative, Thomas. What will you think of next?
I'll create a day just for great moms like you.
THOMAS EDISON'S MOM WAS VERY SUPPORTIVE OF HIM AND WAS HAPPY TO BE THE ---

Now arrange the circled letters to form the surprise answer, as suggested by the above cartoon.

Print answer here

JUMBLE®

Unscramble these six Jumbles, one letter to each square, to form six ordinary words.

HHNEYP

LYUPLE

CANYEG

AOTTTO

GRINIO

FERYEL

I bet you know these roads like the back of your hand. Over.
10-4. Forty years of driving loads and I'm not looking to park it anytime soon.
HE'D BEEN A TRUCK DRIVER FOR YEARS AND WOULD RETIRE A TRUCK DRIVER. HE WAS ---

Now arrange the circled letters to form the surprise answer, as suggested by the above cartoon.

Print answer here

PUZZLE

173

JUMBLE®

Unscramble these six Jumbles, one letter to each square, to form six ordinary words.

MSCOUT

TALYNE

CLOLEA

RNHUCC

FISYTH

LONEOD

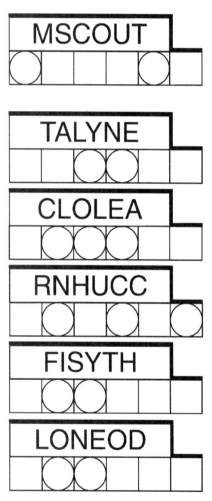

Bless you! There's a cold going around.
May I have a tissue?

MANY OF THE COMMUTERS HEADING INTO THE STATION HAD COLDS. TOGETHER, THEY RODE THE ---

Now arrange the circled letters to form the surprise answer, as suggested by the above cartoon.

Print answer here

“◯◯◯◯◯-◯◯◯◯” ◯◯◯◯◯◯

JUMBLE®

Unscramble these six Jumbles, one letter to each square, to form six ordinary words.

RRNDEE

NWHERC

JUOFLY

TENNYI

DOYHUG

NDIVEA

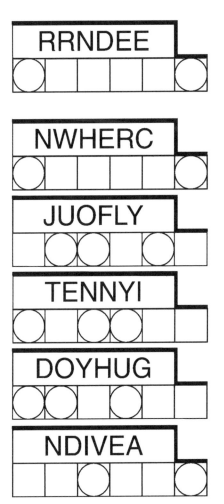

Then he turned into a human! I'm not kidding! He was wearing a tuxedo and started biting this woman on the neck!
THE BAT WAS TELLING AN INTERESTING STORY, AND THE OTHER BATS ---

Now arrange the circled letters to form the surprise answer, as suggested by the above cartoon.

Print answer here

PUZZLE

175

JUMBLE®

Unscramble these six Jumbles, one letter to each square, to form six ordinary words.

RUVEIT

DIETEX

LPOLGA

SDOYHD

KMABER

NARENM

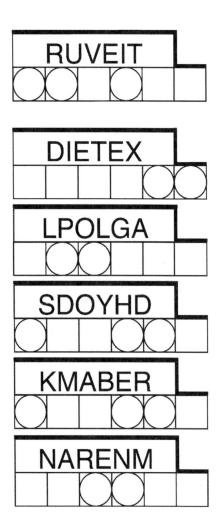

I can only carry two, but I'd love some for the whole family.
We can carry them to your house.
Free of charge.
Ladybug Lemonade Sale 50 cents

WHEN IT CAME TO SELLING LEMONADE, THE GIRLS WERE PREPARED TO ---

Now arrange the circled letters to form the surprise answer, as suggested by the above cartoon.

Print answer here

PUZZLE

176

JUMBLE®

Unscramble these six Jumbles, one letter to each square, to form six ordinary words.

TOONMI

CBSTIE

AURROP

FENDIE

OPLYFP

TLEKTE

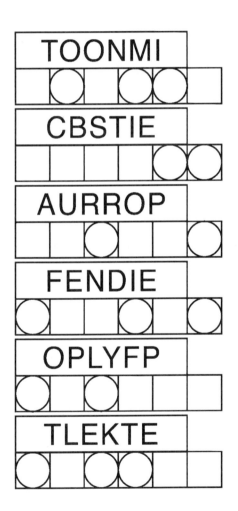

I guess they don't mind us not taking cash anymore.
I knew these kids wouldn't mind. I thought it would work, and it did.
Shirt Shack
Just tap your card here.
No problem.
$25.00
Shirt Shack
NO LONGER ACCEPTING CASH WAS A GOOD IDEA, AND THE STORE OWNER ---

Now arrange the circled letters to form the surprise answer, as suggested by the above cartoon.

Print answer here

JUMBLE®

Unscramble these six Jumbles, one letter to each square, to form six ordinary words.

SBYILU

MYNZEE

SMTACO

TODPET

GREDDE

DICINT

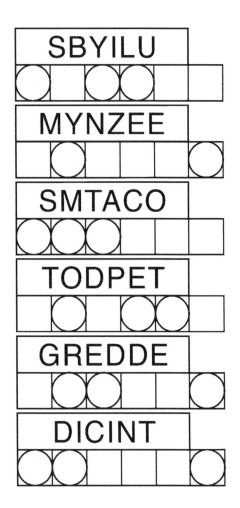

I can't believe these are 2,000 years old.
I can't wait to show our family all of these photos.
WILL THE ACROPOLIS BE A TOURIST ATTRACTION IN ANOTHER 2,000 YEARS? ---

Now arrange the circled letters to form the surprise answer, as suggested by the above cartoon.

Print answer here

PUZZLE

178

JUMBLE®

Unscramble these six Jumbles, one letter to each square, to form six ordinary words.

GLIPTH

NSUIEW

MIEILS

NNNAOC

MYFIAN

HRWATT

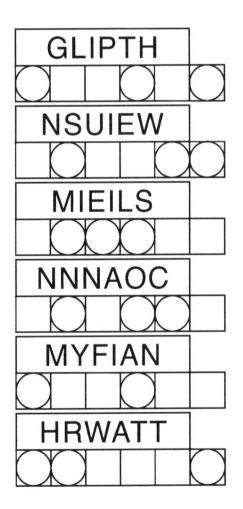

Nice goal! That's a good way to start!
SUDOKUS 0
10:17
JUMBLERS 1
JUMBLE

THE TEAM THAT SCORED THE FIRST GOAL WAS AHEAD ---

Now arrange the circled letters to form the surprise answer, as suggested by the above cartoon.

Print answer here

◯◯ ◯◯◯◯ ◯◯◯◯◯ ◯◯ THE ◯◯◯◯

PUZZLE

179

JUMBLE®

Unscramble these six Jumbles, one letter to each square, to form six ordinary words.

ASCUBA

NCBOKE

KLNEER

WELTLA

MIRHET

SCOYTK

You really got me thinking — we need to practice after five and in the mornings.
I'll move my schedule around.
I'll let Mum know we'll be missing dinners.
WHEN RAY DAVIES AND HIS BROTHER DAVE FORMED THEIR BAND IN 1964, THEY HAD TO ---

Now arrange the circled letters to form the surprise answer, as suggested by the above cartoon.

Print answer here

PUZZLE

180

JUMBLE®

Unscramble these six Jumbles, one letter to each square, to form six ordinary words.

AIFURN

DSOWMI

CODROT

TULOTE

NLAVAD

DHYYAE

You know I'm going to win, don't you?
SCRABBLE CHAMPIONSHIP
Don't make promises you can't keep.
The Champ sounds confident.
I'll stick to being Jumble champ.
THE RETURNING SCRABBLE CHAMPION GUARANTEED ANOTHER VICTORY BY SAYING ---

Now arrange the circled letters to form the surprise answer, as suggested by the above cartoon.

Print answer here

Answers

1. **Jumbles:** TRULY BAKED JERSEY NIPPLE
Answer: What the audience gave him when he was expecting cheers—JEERS
2. **Jumbles:** ALIVE YOUTH UNWISE COMEDY
Answer: What the marriage counselor hoped to give his clients—A GOOD "WED-UCATION"
3. **Jumbles:** CHALK FUZZY BEAUTY IRONIC
Answer: What a successful borrower has to have a good sense of—"TOUCH"
4. **Jumbles:** SANDY UNWED RUBBER JURIST
Answer: What a dude sometimes becomes after marriage—"SUB-DUED"
5. **Jumbles:** KNACK CUBIC WINTRY FIASCO
Answer: What conceit might be a form of—"I-STRAIN"
6. **Jumbles:** HARPY PAGAN JOYOUS ATTACH
Answer: What they called that skid row gym—THE "PAUNCH" SHOP
7. **Jumbles:** SQUAW CHEEK HANDLE NEARBY
Answer: How a conformist usually does things—THE "HERD" WAY
8. **Jumbles:** SQUAB ABBOT ENDURE BRUTAL
Answer: What you might call a guy who never pays what he owes—A "DEBT" BEAT
9. **Jumbles:** SKIMP KEYED VANITY FOSSIL
Answer: How some creatures "multiply"—BY "DIVISION"
10. **Jumbles:** KETCH FRANC ENZYME FINALE
Answer: What is a young man going to be after he reaches eighteen?—NINETEEN
11. **Jumbles:** TROTH ENTRY JAGUAR REBUKE
Answer: What that story about the onion crop was—A TEARJERKER
12. **Jumbles:** SNARL FLOUT TREATY ALBINO
Answer: It's better to love a short guy than this—NOT A TALL
13. **Jumbles:** SWOON GASSY NEGATE FARINA
Answer: The main course at the comedians' annual banquet—THE "ROAST"
14. **Jumbles:** LLAMA PURGE KIMONO FEMALE
Answer: What the baseball that hit the dentist's office was—THE "PANE" KILLER
15. **Jumbles:** EXUDE BULLY SCENIC JARGON
Answer: It takes good manners to put up with this—BAD ONES
16. **Jumbles:** BRAWL WHINE RAMROD SPEEDY
Answer: For a conscientious dieter this should be sufficient—A WORD TO THE "WIDES"
17. **Jumbles:** SOOTY APRON BOTTLE PLEDGE
Answer: What the successful author's novel had—A "PLOT" OF GOLD
18. **Jumbles:** ONION SNOWY VALUED INVENT
Answer: When the viola player disturbed his neighbors late at night, he was arrested for this—A "VIOLA-TION"
19. **Jumbles:** FINNY PANIC GOSPEL CABANA
Answer: A person who seldom pays frequently finds that this is what his life style does—"PAYS"
20. **Jumbles:** LOFTY ABIDE SLOGAN TUSSLE
Answer: What the model thought her career was—AT A "STANDSTILL"
21. **Jumbles:** MEALY INEPT SLOUCH FORMAL
Answer: What he got from remarriage—A NEW "LEASH" ON LIFE
22. **Jumbles:** WEIGH GNARL BANDIT FICKLE
Answer: Whether it rained or not the weather caster was this most of the time—ALL WET
23. **Jumbles:** BLOAT DOWDY ELIXIR INHALE
Answer: Another name for a yawn—A HOLE MADE BY A BORE
24. **Jumbles:** CHESS DECAY FILLET IMMUNE
Answer: What he called those songs he composed in bed—SHEET MUSIC
25. **Jumbles:** CANAL PRUNE GENTRY EGOISM
Answer: It takes more than this to pay an acupuncturist's bill—PIN MONEY
26. **Jumbles:** YODEL CAPON ZEALOT JUMPER
Answer: That reckless chauffeur must have had a license to drive—PEOPLE CRAZY
27. **Jumbles:** SKULK ARMOR ENTAIL BLOODY
Answer: What would you expect to hear from a two-headed monster?—DOUBLE-TALK
28. **Jumbles:** OCCUR FOCUS BOUNTY CRAYON
Answer: What his pal the skeleton was—A BONY CRONY
29. **Jumbles:** AWOKE OLDER STIGMA FROZEN
Answer: A diplomat should know how far to go before he does this—GOES TOO FAR
30. **Jumbles:** SWOOP BLESS FAULTY INDOOR
Answer: Why the mummy had to visit a shrink—HE WAS ALL WOUND UP
31. **Jumbles:** BOOTH AROMA GRISLY SPORTY
Answer: What Dracula's baby liked to hear at bedtime—A GORY STORY
32. **Jumbles:** AVAIL OWING SNAPPY TYPING
Answer: What was the confirmed bachelor's single thought?—STAYING THAT WAY
33. **Jumbles:** FEIGN BANAL SYSTEM HELPER
Answer: Why the magician hired her as his assistant—SHE WAS HIS HALF-SISTER
34. **Jumbles:** WHEEL LUSTY BEATEN DEFILE
Answer: What junior said about the game, after mom made him a new baseball uniform—IT'S ALL "SEWED" UP
35. **Jumbles:** EATEN ARDOR DECENT PHYSIC
Answer: A driver is a guy who forgets that he used to be this—A PEDESTRIAN
36. **Jumbles:** BRASS MERCY SNITCH UPHELD
Answer: If a man married a woman with a title of nobility, what would he be called?—HER HUSBAND
37. **Jumbles:** BOOTH OWING UNHOLY FERVID
Answer: Apparently the easiest habits to break are the ones that are this—GOOD FOR YOU
38. **Jumbles:** DRYLY JUICY UNPACK BROGUE
Answer: What you might do when you read a good horror story—"CURDLE" UP WITH IT
39. **Jumbles:** IGLOO DITTO BEDECK JITNEY
Answer: What the inmates called their library—THE BOOKIE JOINT
40. **Jumbles:** BORAX LEAFY DEAFEN EXODUS
Answer: He was told to eat more seafood, so now he eats every time he does this—SEE FOOD
41. **Jumbles:** MAJOR VOCAL TRUISM PALATE
Answer: The sum total of our national debt is this—"SOME TOTAL!"
42. **Jumbles:** CLOTH SAUTE WHITEN AROUSE
Answer: They kept "minutes" at that meeting but managed to do this—WASTE HOURS
43. **Jumbles:** PANIC YIELD HALLOW FESTAL
Answer: If you don't want your dog to get run over, buy him this—A NEW "LEASH" ON LIFE
44. **Jumbles:** PROVE ROBOT QUARRY MARMOT
Answer: What all that gossip at the boarding house amounted to—ROOMER RUMOR

45. **Jumbles:** PAGAN WOMEN SEPTIC LADING
Answer: What he said when he bought her that new bikini—IT'S THE LEAST I CAN DO

46. **Jumbles:** CROAK YEARN QUORUM ANYHOW
Answer: What do doctors take to get rid of the flu?—YOUR MONEY

47. **Jumbles:** TEPID FRAME PICNIC CASHEW
Answer: She robbed her husband of his peace of mind by constantly giving him this—A PIECE OF HERS

48. **Jumbles:** UTTER WAFER THRUSH FIZZLE
Answer: At a bargain counter, this is what you get—WHAT YOU "SEIZE" ("sees")

49. **Jumbles:** LOGIC PRINT UNCOIL STYMIE
Answer: Some politicians could help their country by getting this—OUT OF POLITICS

50. **Jumbles:** WIPED ABYSS FECUND MAGPIE
Answer: How to open your mouth in a way that might make others shut theirs—YAWN

51. **Jumbles:** WHINE TAKEN QUAINT PUSHER
Answer: A few of those cheeses have this—QUITE A "PHEW"

52. **Jumbles:** WAGER CHOKE FLORAL TAWDRY
Answer: What a bird dog might be trained for hunting in—"FOWL" WEATHER

53. **Jumbles:** OUTDO AISLE BABOON TIPTOE
Answer: Never lend money to this guy!—A "DEBT" BEAT

54. **Jumbles:** CATCH GOING VELVET BEWAIL
Answer: A date is something you must break when you this—HAVE TWO

55. **Jumbles:** HABIT PAPER RACIAL TURGID
Answer: A young person might improve his eyesight when he gets this—A HAIRCUT

56. **Jumbles:** ADULT GUESS CORNEA UNSOLD
Answer: What he said his wife's reasoning largely was—"SOUND"

57. **Jumbles:** SHEEP GLOVE STODGY HIDING
Answer: What his handicap in golf was—HIS HONESTY

58. **Jumbles:** METAL CRACK VARIED KETTLE
Answer: There was a lot of this in the waiting room of the employment agency—"IDLE" TALK

59. **Jumbles:** ADMIT FANCY DISMAL TRUDGE
Answer: What the lawyer who joined the nudist colony never had—A "SUIT" AGAIN

60. **Jumbles:** LEGAL EJECT JUNKET HOMING
Answer: He who laughs last probably doesn't this—GET THE JOKE

61. **Jumbles:** COVEY MANGE KIDNAP VIRTUE
Answer: He married her for her looks, but not this—THE KIND SHE OFTEN GAVE HIM

62. **Jumbles:** BANAL VAGUE FAUCET SHAKEN
Answer: What you can't make on a slow horse—A FAST BUCK

63. **Jumbles:** POUCH TARRY SECOND HICCUP
Answer: Another name for that reducing salon—THE "PAUNCH" SHOP

64. **Jumbles:** CRANK SHINY TIMELY FEWEST
Answer: Often dropped but seldom picked up—HINTS

65. **Jumbles:** AFOOT MAXIM VACANT SHANTY
Answer: What they called that wealthy playboy—"CASH-ANOVA"

66. **Jumbles:** PYLON TWEET EXHALE DIGEST
Answer: What the sentry at the army kitchen kept—HIS EYES "PEELED"

67. **Jumbles:** DRAMA BASIN STOOGE UNEASY
Answer: Is she a good dressmaker?—SO IT "SEAMS"

68. **Jumbles:** NEEDY DUNCE FITFUL CHROME
Answer: He was often a friend of the owner which is why he got everything—ON THE "CUFF"

69. **Jumbles:** CHAMP BUILT KILLER POETRY
Answer: What they called those two porcupines—A PRICKLY "PAIR"

70. **Jumbles:** GNOME JOUST MAKEUP SAVAGE
Answer: Sticks to one thing and hopefully gets there—A STAMP

71. **Jumbles:** ODIUM BANJO CIRCUS HAPPEN
Answer: What to tie up that grand with—PIANO "CHORDS"

72. **Jumbles:** BERTH GLORY SWIVEL HOURLY
Answer: What the rodeo performer does in order to impress others—THROWS THE BULL

73. **Jumbles:** POISE GRIMY CANINE TORRID
Answer: He was so lazy he wouldn't even exercise this—DISCRETION

74. **Jumbles:** RAINY BIPED ABOUND EMBARK
Answer: When rock-'n'-roll was first introduced, some old-timers said it should be this—"BAND"

75. **Jumbles:** REBEL CROON SECEDE TRUANT
Answer: When will the mail arrive?—SOONER OR "LETTER"

76. **Jumbles:** CURIO BANDY PREACH MYSELF
Answer: What dry-as-dust people never seem to do—DRY UP

77. **Jumbles:** PRONE ENVOY CHORUS RANCID
Answer: What kids get a big bang out of—THE SCREEN DOOR

78. **Jumbles:** GROIN HYENA KITTEN RECTOR
Answer: They've improved the trains to Washington so that the politicians can now do this—GET ON THE RIGHT TRACK

79. **Jumbles:** BEGOT ENSUE NEARBY RADIUM
Answer: She used to be afraid of mice until she finally decided to do this—MARRY ONE

80. **Jumbles:** WHILE AFTER BUSILY AMBUSH
Answer: What's that underground movement that's going on in many cities?—THE SUBWAY

81. **Jumbles:** KITTY BAGGY TURNIP MATURE
Answer: One sure way to beat the stock market—JUST "BEAT IT!"

82. **Jumbles:** LEAVE PAUSE FERRET HARROW
Answer: What a rainy day is for a cab driver—"FARE" WEATHER

83. **Jumbles:** VALET HURRY UPWARD SUBMIT
Answer: The pessimist was hanging around the delicatessen store because he was waiting for this—THE "WURST"

84. **Jumbles:** BEFIT PUTTY HEAVEN FALLOW
Answer: What a good police dog might put—TEETH INTO THE LAW

85. **Jumbles:** DOUSE BLOOD LEEWAY RATIFY
Answer: Every time he has an argument with his wife, this happens—WORDS "FLAIL" HIM

86. **Jumbles:** STOKE AIDED CENSUS SOLACE
Answer: What the ship's doctors generally do—"SEE SICKNESS"

87. **Jumbles:** FORAY SYLPH UNLOAD LARYNX
Answer: If you become addicted to wrestling, it might do this—GET A HOLD ON YOU

88. **Jumbles:** GRIEF HOUSE TOTTER NUANCE
Answer: He married a rich wife, so he never had to pay anything—except this—ATTENTION

89. **Jumbles:** GRAVE POKED BUTTER SOCIAL
Answer: What the canine member of the Boy Scouts was called—A "BEAGLE" SCOUT

90. **Jumbles:** ITCHY KETCH FIGURE TACKLE
Answer: He thought he was a wit, and most of them said he was this—HALF-RIGHT

91. **Jumbles:** BLANK WRATH AGENCY JOSTLE
Answer: What the robber tried to do after he stole all the money—"STEAL" AWAY

92. **Jumbles:** THINK POWER JURIST SCURVY
Answer: "Does your wife pick your clothes?"—"JUST THE POCKETS"

93. **Jumbles:** VIPER NOISY PEPSIN LICHEN
Answer: He tried to kiss her, but she'd have this—
NONE OF HIS LIP

94. **Jumbles:** BASIC QUILT MELODY CARPET
Answer: What lace should never be—OUT OF "P-LACE"

95. **Jumbles:** RIGOR NEWSY GENIUS RARITY
Answer: Bigamy is when two—"RITES" MAKE A WRONG

96. **Jumbles:** CRAZE ABIDE TYPIST BLOUSE
Answer: What ignorance at the beach is—"BLISS-TER"

97. **Jumbles:** HOARD PIKER TONGUE INHALE
Answer: Why the burlesque queen decided to run for office—
SHE HAD NOTHING TO HIDE

98. **Jumbles:** DOILY JUROR VIOLIN PHYSIC
Answer: What happens every time he turns over a new leaf?—
IT'S POISON IVY

99. **Jumbles:** BRAVE COLON DELUGE ADAGIO
Answer: This might help a gambler win a good deal of chips—
A GOOD DEAL

100. **Jumbles:** NOVEL MINUS UPTOWN GULLET
Answer: Another name for money that's gained through inheritance—"WILL-GOTTEN"

101. **Jumbles:** COCOA ROBIN BYWORD LAGOON
Answer: What the accordionist's concert was—
LONG DRAWN OUT

102. **Jumbles:** DEMON RUSTY SKEWER FETISH
Answer: When you try to wash a small kid he's apt to do this—
SHRINK FROM IT

103. **Jumbles:** UNITY SCOUR BAKING CAMPER
Answer: Some aging thespians might find it difficult to do this—ACT THEIR AGE

104. **Jumbles:** ERUPT HELLO UNSAID RARELY
Answer: One way to get ahead and stay ahead is to do this—
USE YOUR HEAD

105. **Jumbles:** BOGUS QUASH MUSKET CLERGY
Answer: What legal "tender" might be when you don't have it—"TOUGH"

106. **Jumbles:** HUSKY AGILE BEAUTY IMBIBE
Answer: In those days a woman would raise a hem in order to do this—GET A "HIM"

107. **Jumbles:** AORTA CARGO POWDER JUNIOR
Answer: Another name for a cloudburst—A "DROWN POUR"

108. **Jumbles:** CLEFT OAKEN FINISH INFUSE
Answer: It was off-season for fishing, which is why the sheriff made it this—"OFF-FISH-AL" (official)

109. **Jumbles:** DERBY CRAWL BEAVER LAYMAN
Answer: What the bank robber got when the security system sounded—"ALARMED"

110. **Jumbles:** EAGLE FAIRY LANCER POPLAR
Answer: What to do when the barometer falls—
REPLACE THE NAIL

111. **Jumbles:** HAVOC BLURB DONKEY PALACE
Answer: The trail the twins walked on had ended, so they decided to—DOUBLE BACK

112. **Jumbles:** STOMP RIVER FONDUE PEANUT
Answer: When they figured out how to get syrup from maples, it was—"TREE-MENDOUS"

113. **Jumbles:** BUILD GLOAT SPRUCE JUSTLY
Answer: When Neil deGrasse Tyson explains a star formation he does a—STELLAR JOB

114. **Jumbles:** MIGHT THIRD PEDDLE FINISH
Answer: The tourists thought they'd be able to visit Big Ben, but they couldn't—FIND THE TIME

115. **Jumbles:** CARGO FRESH CATNIP INFAMY
Answer: George VI's new shoes were causing him much pain. They were—FIT FOR "ACHING"

116. **Jumbles:** ESSAY TRUNK ROOKIE PACKET
Answer: To write down their golf scores, the cartoonist used—
PEN STROKES

117. **Jumbles:** TUMMY WEAVE PROVEN SHRIMP
Answer: He was a cook in the military and was proud to—
SERVE IN THE ARMY

118. **Jumbles:** NOISY ICING HERBAL HOTTER
Answer: She loved losing weight and seeing the pounds vanish—INTO THIN AIR

119. **Jumbles:** LOUSY PANDA HAZARD TUNNEL
Answer: Sleep Hollow's infamous horseman was able to help his tug-o-war team—PULL AHEAD

120. **Jumbles:** CLANG BERRY SAFETY IMPOSE
Answer: Questioning the dog about the ripped-up newspaper was—"RE-TORE-ICAL"

121. **Jumbles:** CATCH ITCHY PARLOR EMERGE
Answer: When Nate Sherman started Midas Muffler in 1956, it was a great—"CAR-REAR" CHOICE

122. **Jumbles:** PATIO DOUBT RIPPLE TWELVE
Answer: Upon retirement, they build a mountaintop dream home and—LIVED IT UP

123. **Jumbles:** WORLD BOGUS FIRMLY ENOUGH
Answer: He challenged him to arm wrestle. Now they just needed some—ELBOW ROOM

124. **Jumbles:** ROUGH INEPT LOTION MIDDAY
Answer: He paid big bucks for the race horse and had a lot—
RIDING ON IT

125. **Jumbles:** AWAIT THUMP SURVEY CATCHY
Answer: When they used freshly-picked peaches to make the pies, it was—THE PITS

126. **Jumbles:** TWIRL WEDGE SMOOTH GOVERN
Answer: Jim Morrison and his band had so many fans, it was difficult to—GET IN THE DOORS

127. **Jumbles:** RISKY SWOON LUNACY INLAND
Answer: To enter the cave with the low entrance, they would need all their—DUCKS IN A ROW

128. **Jumbles:** HUTCH FORCE SEESAW PELLET
Answer: When the chicken converted the old sports car into a helicopter, she—FLEW THE "COUPE"

129. **Jumbles:** SCOUT HELLO TRENDY ATRIUM
Answer: The ancient deli used the abacus as its—
MEAT COUNTER

130. **Jumbles:** RIGOR GAUGE WEALTH FATHER
Answer: The battle for business between the sod sellers was a—
TURF WAR

131. **Jumbles:** ROBIN LOUSY TENANT ASTRAY
Answer: How many guards protect the New York Harbor statue? They're not—AT LIBERTY TO SAY

132. **Jumbles:** DECAY BLAND OBLONG VALLEY
Answer: When Chuck Yeager broke the sound barrier, he went—
ABOVE AND BEYOND

133. **Jumbles:** LARVA DRAWN POTENT BUSILY
Answer: The Earth orbits the sun—ALL YEAR ROUND

134. **Jumbles:** EMPTY EVENT SPIRAL IMPACT
Answer: The tennis match would begin—AT A SET TIME

135. **Jumbles:** TINGE SKUNK UTOPIA TIMELY
Answer: When the elephants worked together, they were—
"MULTI-TUSKING"

136. **Jumbles:** GOURD FAULT LAVISH BUNDLE
Answer: When the Beatles were asked if they wanted to tour America, they were—ALL "FOUR" IT

137. **Jumbles:** TOPAZ GUESS TIGHTS NOVICE
Answer: After the hypodermic needle was perfected, doctors were ready to—GIVE IT A SHOT

138. **Jumbles:** SPOIL ONION MIRROR TAUGHT
Answer: The retired doctor bought a hotel and became a—"ROOM-ATOLOGIST"

139. **Jumbles:** IMPEL FORGO ODDEST NUANCE
Answer: When Edison invented the phonograph, there was no doubt that he was—OF SOUND MIND

140. **Jumbles:** LOGIC TWINE REDUCE JABBER
Answer: When another coffee shop opened next door, there was—TROUBLE BREWING

141. **Jumbles:** NOTCH FOCAL DECENT JACKAL
Answer: When he applied for a patent on his pull-tab invention, the patent office said—CAN DO

142. **Jumbles:** HEDGE IRONY LOUNGE VOYAGE
Answer: NASCAR star Kevin Harvick loves golf and particularly enjoys a—LONG DRIVE

143. **Jumbles:** RAZOR FLUID FUNGUS JESTER
Answer: The two houses for lease looked alike, but it was easy to spot the—"DIFFER-RENTS"

144. **Jumbles:** OCTET VOICE KNOTTY FATHOM
Answer: The new bistro was the most elegant in town, and diners—TOOK A FANCY TO IT

145. **Jumbles:** INPUT FOAMY LAWYER NOODLE
Answer: The sun has been coming up in the east every morning since the—DAWN OF TIME

146. **Jumbles:** WEIGH OFTEN FAULTY FEEBLE
Answer: With the oil field depleted, they shut down operations. But the owner was—WELL OFF

147. **Jumbles:** PAUSE HUMID COLDER MOMENT
Answer: With dirty clothes everywhere, her attempt to clean her room was being—HAMPERED

148. **Jumbles:** WATCH GRIND TIMELY UNTOLD
Answer: When Harry and Meghan splashed each other on their honeymoon, it was a—ROYAL "WETTING"

149. **Jumbles:** CHAIR BROOM FRUGAL ELDEST
Answer: When asked to help with his Independence Day cookout, his friends—CAME "FOURTH"

150. **Jumbles:** SALSA FENCE MINING FORBID
Answer: Running up a hillside can be great exercise if you are—SO INCLINED

151. **Jumbles:** GRAPH WHARF DEPUTY BABOON
Answer: Her detailed explanation of how the toll money would be used was a—"THOROUGH-FARE"

152. **Jumbles:** LASSO GRIME HOLLOW SAFARI
Answer: When asked if he was happy to spot land, he said—I "SHORE" AM

153. **Jumbles:** GUMBO GAUGE BALLAD ADJOIN
Answer: The carpenter was very muscular, and his admirers noticed his—GOOD BUILD

154. **Jumbles:** SOUPY PRONG SNAZZY KITTEN
Answer: When he failed the driving portion of his driver's test, he was in a—NO PASSING ZONE

155. **Jumbles:** FOYER LINER PADDLE JIGSAW
Answer: The inventor of the saddle had the—"RIDE" IDEA

156. **Jumbles:** EMCEE HIKER ABSURD PUSHUP
Answer: He longed to be a bounty hunter and planned to—PURSUE HIS DREAM

157. **Jumbles:** DEITY GLINT GLOSSY TENANT
Answer: The shady pharmaceutical executive's profits were—ILL-GOTTEN GAINS

158. **Jumbles:** CACHE MAIZE STENCH STEREO
Answer: After the outfielder ended the 15-inning game, he was ready to—CATCH SOME Z'S

159. **Jumbles:** SIXTY BERTH BRONCO JINGLE
Answer: When it came to showing off his ability, the pool player was a—BIG SHOT

160. **Jumbles:** FRONT DOUSE CLOSED GLOBAL
Answer: When the space probe approached Pluto, mission control said—SO FAR, SO GOOD

161. **Jumbles:** HONCHO DETECT LAVISH OPPOSE IMPACT HOTTER
Answer: He was beginning to accept the fact that he was a ghost. The other ghosts said—THAT'S THE SPIRIT

162. **Jumbles:** INWARD SUDDEN SPLINT ASSIGN INHALE EMBODY
Answer: The recluse extracted gold without any help and liked to—"MINE" HIS OWN BUSINESS

163. **Jumbles:** SESAME SUMMER DRIVER SAVORY AVENUE SYSTEM
Answer: The poetry competition featured—VERSES VERSUS VERSES

164. **Jumbles:** IRONIC FEISTY HOURLY GRUMPY OFFEND ORIGIN
Answer: A zero doesn't have any value because it's—GOOD FOR NOTHING

165. **Jumbles:** OBLONG MORALE SWIVEL ACCENT EYEFUL KNOTTY
Answer: When the baby's first words were "da-da…da-da," the father exclaimed—NOW YOU'RE TALIKIN'!

166. **Jumbles:** HYPHEN EMERGE HINDER STUFFY DEARLY GLOSSY
Answer: Santa could see the pride his helpers took in their work. It was clear by their—HIGH "ELF"-ESTEEM

167. **Jumbles:** HELMET EMBLEM PLURAL DRAFTY NOBODY ATTEND
Answer: To raise money quickly, the athlete sold his Olympic gold by putting the—"PEDDLE" TO THE "MEDAL"

168. **Jumbles:** HUDDLE INWARD EASILY TETHER MAINLY DAMAGE
Answer: When asked when she thought the dress would be finished, she—HEMMED AND HAWED

169. **Jumbles:** ONWARD EXPORT SAILOR TANDEM NEPHEW OCCUPY
Answer: For the bunnies to deliver the Easter eggs together, it required—"CO-HOP-ERATION"

170. **Jumbles:** GENTLE EXODUS ACIDIC CURFEW PANTRY HIGHLY
Answer: She loved the wording of his marriage proposal and thought it—HAD A NICE RING TO IT

171. **Jumbles:** NOTION FEWEST MOTIVE HOURLY MOTION DEPICT
Answer: Thomas Edison's mom was very supportive of him and was happy to be the—MOTHER OF INVENTION

172. **Jumbles:** HYPHEN AGENCY ORIGIN PULLEY TATTOO FREELY
Answer: He'd been a truck driver for years and would retire a truck driver. He was—IN IT FOR THE LONG HAUL

173. **Jumbles:** CUSTOM LOCALE SHIFTY NEATLY CRUNCH NOODLE
Answer: Many of the commuters heading into the station had colds. Together they rode the—"ACHOO-CHOO" TRAIN

174. **Jumbles:** RENDER JOYFUL DOUGHY WRENCH NINETY INVADE
Answer: The bat was telling an interesting story, and the other bats—HUNG ON EVERY WORD

175. **Jumbles:** VIRTUE GALLOP EMBARK EXITED SHODDY MANNER
Answer: When it came to selling lemonade, the girls were prepared to—STAND AND DELIVER

176. **Jumbles:** MOTION UPROAR FLOPPY BISECT DEFINE KETTLE
Answer: No longer accepting cash was a good idea, and the store owner—TOOK CREDIT FOR IT

177. **Jumbles:** BUSILY MASCOT DREDGE ENZYME POTTED INDICT
Answer: Will the Acropolis be a tourist attraction in another 2,000 years?—IT REMAINS TO BE SEEN

178. **Jumbles:** PLIGHT SIMILE INFAMY UNWISE CANNON THWART
Answer: The team that scored the first goal was ahead—AT THIS POINT IN THE GAME

179. **Jumbles:** ABACUS KERNEL HERMIT BECKON WALLET STOCKY
Answer: When Ray Davies and his brother Dave formed their band in 1964, they had to—WORK OUT THE KINKS

180. **Jumbles:** UNFAIR DOCTOR VANDAL WISDOM OUTLET HEYDAY
Answer: The returning Scrabble champion guaranteed another victory by saying—YOU HAVE MY WORD ON IT